Praise for *The Beginner's Guide to Cooperative Learning*

Jakob Werdelin and Drew Howard have produced an excellent guide to Cooperative Learning that provides teachers with a coherent philosophy and a detailed structure for bringing it to life in the classroom. Far beyond many teachers' view of 'group work', the CLIPs concept is clearly defined with lots of examples. Most importantly, the authors have pitched high, insisting that all their suggested activities deliver the rigour required for PIES – the four requirements of positive interdependence, individual accountability, equal participation and simultaneous interaction which ensure that all children are participating, thinking and learning. This is great to see. Jakob and Drew's audacious claim that Cooperative Learning is the solution to everything might be hard to accept, but nonetheless it's an interesting challenge to explore and, as well as being practical as a handy guide, this book makes an engaging and compelling case for more Cooperative Learning in schools.

Tom Sherrington, author of *The Learning Rainforest* **and** *Teaching WalkThrus*

Forget everything you think you know about collaborative learning and the silly prog–trad debates which cloud the issue. This brilliant, powerful book seeks to redefine what Cooperative Learning is and – *spoiler alert* – it is not disorganised group work.

Written in an engaging and humorous yet authoritative and knowledgeable way, it defines the key concepts and explains the action steps which can be put in place to transform learning in our schools. After the theoretical and practical grounding of the first two chapters, each chapter thereafter is like a stand-alone unit, which can be dipped into as and when required. What's more, the book features a variety of different subject-specific examples and covers a wide range of topics, including how Cooperative Learning links to Rosenshine's principles, getting your teaching assistant involved and a real-life case study of how a school embedded the approach. The authors provide a step-by-step manual which will equip any teacher from any phase with all the tools to get impactful Cooperative Learning up and running in their classroom.

Haili Hughes, Head of Education, IRIS Connect, Senior Lecturer, University of Sunderland, author and speaker

What I gathered very quickly is that Cooperative Learning is a simple yet incredibly powerful approach whereby learners are carefully trained to interact with one another and their learning in such a way that they do the hard work while also learning content quicker and gaining essential social skills. What's not to like?

Stephen Chapman, Managing Director, Dragonfly Training Ltd

Tackling the often misunderstood and poorly applied principles of Cooperative Learning, this detailed and evidence-informed book sits astride traditionalist and progressive dichotomies, and provides proven step-by-step structures and strategies that have the potential to enhance and even transform your practice. An essential guide for anyone interested in fostering interdependence, accountability, participation and interaction within the classroom.

Jonathan Lear, teacher, speaker and author of *The Monkey-Proof Box*

The Beginner's Guide to Cooperative Learning is for anyone who, like me, has been wondering just how to connect subject content with the art of being human. If you want great results *and* resilient capable young people who can hold their own in a conversation, take responsibility and engage intelligently with other people, this is the book for you. One of the most fascinating things, I find, is the necessary intimate connection between direct instruction from a capable teacher and the social construction that processes and integrates what has been taught through oracy and higher-level thinking.

This book does not fit into the traditional or progressive category in any way, shape or form; like all good teaching, it transcends simple lines in the sand. So, don't let the title scare you if you are a traditionalist. If you are a fan of Barak Rosenshine you will not only enjoy the dedicated chapter on him, viewed through the lens of Tom Sherrington's neat streamlining, but you will also recognise his principles in the most unlikely places on every page of highly child-centred learning in this book.

Catherine Brentnall, researcher and curriculum development consultant

In this thoughtful and useful book, Jakob and Drew clearly offer the busy classroom teacher the 'how' of Cooperative Learning as well as, importantly, the 'why'. I'm all for any approach and pedagogy that encourages children and young people to find their learning voices, and this book enables the thoughtful teacher to do just that with their classes.

Hywel Roberts, teacher, speaker, writer and humorist

Jakob Werdelin and Drew Howard

The Beginner's Guide to
Cooperative Learning

Make your learners your main teaching resource

Crown House Publishing Limited
www.crownhouse.co.uk

Published by
Crown House Publishing
Crown Buildings, Bancyfelin, Carmarthen, Wales, SA33 5ND, UK
www.crownhouse.co.uk
and
Crown House Publishing Company LLC
PO Box 2223, Williston, VT 05495, USA
www.crownhousepublishing.com

Page 46, Figure 2.4 – Key Stage 2 maths and GCSE history flashcards © HarperCollins Publishers. Available at https://collins.co.uk/pages/revision-collins-ks1-ks2-revision-and-practice-flashcards-resources and https://collins.co.uk/pages/revision-gcse-ages-14-16-collins-gcse-revision-and-practice-flashcards. Used with permission.

Material from Ofsted and Department for Education documents used in this publication have been approved under an Open Government Licence. Please see http://www.nationalarchives.gov.uk/doc/open-government-licence/version/3.

Crown House Publishing has no responsibility for the persistence or accuracy of URLs for external or third-party websites referred to in this publication, and does not guarantee that any content on such websites is, or will remain, accurate or appropriate.

British Library of Cataloguing-in-Publication Data
A catalogue entry for this book is available from the British Library.

Print ISBN 978-178583585-8
Mobi ISBN 978-178583589-6
ePub ISBN 978-178583590-2
ePDF ISBN 978-178583591-9

LCCN 2021945969

Printed and bound in the UK by
Charlesworth Press, Wakefield, West Yorkshire

To the people with whom we have worked.

Contents

Introduction: Cooperative Learning and the COVID Comeback

When we began drafting this book in 2017, our intention was simply to share with colleagues the inner workings of Cooperative Learning at Stalham Academy in Norfolk, and its wider multi-academy trust (MAT), over a number of years. Looking back, 2017 seems a lifetime and a world away. In general terms, of course, Cooperative Learning is always relevant because it is a cost-effective way to promote academic performance and social skills. More specifically to the 2020s, Cooperative Learning is relevant because it effortlessly operationalises key theories underpinning the 2019 Ofsted Inspection Framework. These and many other arguments for the adoption of Cooperative Learning are expounded throughout this book. However, COVID-19 has added entirely new levels of importance, and some degree of urgency, which deserves to be touched on separately.

It is reasonable to say that, in spite of a monumental effort by schools, the pandemic has had a devastating effect on all areas of education. In primary schools alone, the attainment gap has widened by up to 52% during school closures, according to *Schools Week*.[1] Unsurprisingly, learners with lower socio-economic status take the brunt of this blow, and within that group those with language barriers, mental health problems or prior learning difficulties will be affected even more. We can also add to this factors such as race and gender. Beyond this learning gap proper, it is expected that inequality in 'socio-emotional skills' will also increase.[2] Crucially, the pandemic has widened the already stubborn

---

1 J. Dicken, The Cost of Lockdown: Attainment Gap Widens By Up to 52% for Primary Pupils, *Schools Week* (24 July 2020). Available at: https://schoolsweek.co.uk/the-cost-of-lockdown-attainment-gap-widens-by-up-to-52-for-primary-pupils.

2 G. Di Pietro, F. Biagi, P. Costa, Z. Karpiński and J. Mazza, *The Likely Impact of COVID-19 on Education: Reflections Based on the Existing Literature and Recent International Datasets* (Luxembourg: Publications Office of the European Union, 2020), p. 29. Available at: https://publications.jrc.ec.europa.eu/repository/bitstream/JRC121071/jrc121071.pdf.

language gap, with Ofsted warning that children hit hardest are 'regressing in basic skills and learning', including language, communication and oral fluency.[3]

The upshot is that, a decade after the world's last COVID-19 patient has been discharged, the education sector will still be catching up on the general learning loss, as well as an unprecedented gap in social, emotional, cognitive and language skills for a vastly enlarged group of vulnerable learners. If you are like most teaching professionals, tackling all these challenges coherently with a patchwork of individual interventions seems more than overwhelming. But, what if you could find one relatively simple, comprehensive approach – a framework of sorts? You would need an approach that simultaneously re-forms institutional cohesion, tackles emotional and social lockdown fallout *and* increases the volume of learning per lesson to close the gaps. And, this intervention of yours must do these three things for *every* learner regardless of level, race or socio-economic background and must work across *any* subject and age group; it must use your current schemes of work; and it must fit with or enhance any other approaches, while adding as little as humanly possible to teacher workload.

It is our hope that Cooperative Learning can meet all of these requirements.

What's in this book?

Whether you approach this book as a teacher or a leader, this *Beginner's Guide to Cooperative Learning* is a step-by-step manual to get simple, powerful Cooperative Learning up and running in your class or school. The objective is to make the learners responsible for their learning, leaving you free to concentrate on the teaching. Based on best practice developed over many years, it provides precise, detailed instructions to make you an expert practitioner. However, for all its precision, Cooperative Learning is far from prescriptive. Rather, it lets you get on, but get on better, in a way that you are comfortable with, using your own trusted materials and systems. Best of all, it lets you experiment and develop your own practice. Step into the driver's seat and let the kids do the pedalling.

This book does not claim to cover all of the many varying interpretations of the term 'cooperative learning'. Instead, the principles and practices you see here have been applied successfully by ourselves on a wide range of learners in the UK (and through Jakob's

---

3 Ofsted, Children Hardest Hit By COVID-19 Pandemic Are Regressing in Basic Skills and Learning (10 November 2020) [press release]. Available at: https://www.gov.uk/government/news/ofsted-children-hardest-hit-by-covid-19-pandemic-are-regressing-in-basic-skills-and-learning.

international work in other educational cultures). Although the age groups range from children in the early years foundation stage (EYFS) explaining simple shapes, right up to university lecturers elaborating on how to best teach the content of their PhD,[4] the examples and transcripts in this book will focus on Key Stages 1 to 4.

We want this book to work for you. Within reasonable limits, the chapters are designed as stand-alone units, directly accessible as required by your individual needs and interests. However, the chapters marked with asterisks (*) are must-reads for everyone. Aside from the definitions in Chapter 1 and the detailed instructions for roll-out in Chapter 2 (which should be followed stringently!), you may approach this book in a non-linear fashion. Some readers might prioritise context and theory, so may skip forward to the chapters on the relationship between Cooperative Learning and direct instruction or social construction (Chapters 3 and 4). Others might prefer to try out a couple of activities and then review these chapters in light of their experiences.

Of course, as you begin to deploy Cooperative Learning in your classroom, you can dip in and out as the situation demands. Need to get your teaching assistant (TA) on board? Find TAs in Chapter 5 on roles and responsibilities. Need to see the big picture? Learn how one school successfully developed a MAT approach in Chapter 6. Dennis the Menace giving you trouble? You will find him and his kin dealt with in Chapter 8. With this non-linearity in mind, we hope you will forgive some repetition of key points. Its purpose is to allow random snacking.

The following chapter outline is there to help you make these choices. Remember that the chapters marked with asterisks (*) are must-reads for everyone.

Introduction

This chapter provides a bit of context and gives you the reasons why you may wish to read and apply this book, from the perspective of the bigger scheme of things. We suggest reading the first section as a minimum.

---

4   Find out more in this short video interview with Professor Lee Marsden at the University of East Anglia: J. Werdelin, Tertiary in the 21st Century: A Cooperative Learning Toolkit (2015). Available at: https://videos. werdelin.co.uk/#collection/13.

Chapter 1: What is Cooperative Learning? (And Especially What It Isn't)*

A better title might have been 'What *isn't* Cooperative Learning?' Here, we unpick some critical misconceptions and demonstrate how Cooperative Learning negates the politically charged conflict between progressive vs. traditional, student-led vs. teacher-led and so on. We then refer to some research evidence and introduce and define the Cooperative Learning Interaction Pattern (CLIP), which is undoubtedly the most important concept in this book. We also discover how Cooperative Learning relates to some of the research findings that underpin the 2019 Inspection Framework to enlighten your conversation with inspectors.

> The Cooperative Learning Interaction Pattern (CLIP) is undoubtedly the most important concept in this book.

Chapter 2: Catch1Partner – an Exemplary CLIP*

This chapter is the heart of this volume. It is a step-by-step guide to introducing and growing the versatile CLIP dubbed Catch1Partner in your school. Here, you will learn how to facilitate social skills, language acquisition (general and subject specific), revision, metacognition, formative assessment, self-assessment, peer feedback and a whole lot of other things – with relatively little work on your part. Our intention is that by fully mastering the principles of staging and running Catch1Partner in its many forms, you will be ready to apply these skills to any other CLIP (there are more in Appendix A).

Chapter 3: Cooperative Learning and Direct Instruction*

The individual Cooperative Learning activities are in themselves incredibly powerful, but using them at the appropriate time and place in a lesson really takes them to another level. Based on Barak Rosenshine's famous paper 'Principles of Instruction,'[5] this section puts Cooperative Learning into the context of a best practice lesson and drives home Cooperative Learning's dependence on direct instruction.

---

5 B. Rosenshine, Principles of Instruction: Research-Based Strategies That All Teachers Should Know, *American Educator* (spring 2012), 12–19, 39. Available at: https://www.aft.org/sites/default/files/periodicals/Rosenshine.pdf.

Chapter 4: Cooperative Learning and Social Construction

This is a look at the mechanics behind the slick surface of well-executed Cooperative Learning. While not as central to your practical success, it does form a couplet of a sort with the previous chapter on direct instruction.

Chapter 5: The Roles and Responsibilities of Cooperative Learning: What's in It for You and Everyone Else?

What's in it for you? Because Cooperative Learning looks at human beings as the key resource in any situation, everyone has a unique part to play in a Cooperative Learning school, from the head teacher to the TA and right down to the youngest learners.

Chapter 6: The Story of Stalham: A Reflection on Implementation Across a School

Get inspired by finding out how Cooperative Learning played an integral part in moving a disintegrating, headless, freshly converted junior school from special measures to the nation's top 500 league, with happy teachers, children and parents.

Chapter 7: Teaching Materials: The Stuff You Don't Need to Buy

In this chapter you will learn how materials can be used weekly (or even daily) across classes for years on end to achieve different and specific outcomes. Note that revision, which is important enough in its own right, is only one of the more obvious benefits of reusing materials systematically. You will also learn how to adapt materials to tie your school community together in time as well as space. In the long run, time spent planning and resourcing can, and often does, reduce workload over time.

Chapter 8: The Pitfalls of Cooperative Learning – Things That Go 'Bump' in the Classroom*

The problem with turning children into your main classroom resource is that they are human beings, with all that it entails. What if someone just does not want to take part? What if they are teaching each other the wrong thing? This chapter comprises answers to common questions from teachers and school leaders who have trained with us.

Chapter 9: Cooperative Learning and Other Strategies

Many teachers use the same basic structure across many of their lessons. Whether you have your own unique style or follow the guidance from works such as Shaun Allison and Andy Tharby's Making Every Lesson Count series[6] or Tom Sherrington's *Rosenshine's Principles in Action*,[7] Cooperative Learning can slot straight in with what you are doing and strengthen each stage of your lesson. From SOLO taxonomy to Talk for Writing, Cooperative Learning will support, and in most cases enhance, any system in which you have previously invested.

Appendices

Once you have fully mastered Catch1Partner, by following the step-by-step instructions in Chapter 2, you and your learners should have the foundational know-how and experience to start deploying other CLIPs in your class and school, which you will find in Appendix A. We have included some ready-to-photocopy sample teaching materials, tools and guidelines in Appendix B.[8] Appendix C is a checklist of things to watch out for, and Appendix D provides some simple tools for peer and self-reflection (both of these resources are also photocopiable, for your convenience). The quick reference guide in Appendix E unpicks the acronyms used in this book (CLIP? PIES?) and provides a reminder of the four basic rules for staging an activity. Finally, we have included a full activity transcript which may inspire your use of the CLIP Word-Round in Appendix F.

Why read this book?

There are few certainties in life. However, education does seem to have three constants that affect every school from small rural primaries through to huge London colleges: policies change with each new government, money is short and classrooms are full of learners of all shapes and sizes. Based on these constants alone, it makes sense to make your learners your main teaching resource. They are unlikely to disappear anytime soon, they cost

---

6   See, for example, S. Allison and A. Tharby, *Making Every Lesson Count: Six Principles to Support Great Teaching and Learning* (Carmarthen: Crown House Publishing, 2015). To date, there are nine titles in this series.

7   T. Sherrington, *Rosenshine's Principles in Action* (Woodbridge: John Catt Educational, 2019).

8   These are also available to print directly from the internet in a public folder at: https://drive.google.com/drive/folders/1aqfQGiV7VLEMF2NoivlwtUdk1Xe-0uu2 (https://bit.ly/TheBeginnersGuideDownloads).

you nothing, most of them are delivered to your door every morning and their brains are endlessly flexible.

This book is about doing just that: turning each and every learner, regardless of their religious, ethnic or socio-economic background, into a resource – to themselves, to you, to their peers, to their school, to their families, to their local community and to the world at large.

Cooperative Learning sets a stage that can help each learner become a competent and empathic individual, capable of making sound choices and with the natural potential to develop throughout life. And, of crucial importance for your institution, this successful life will be launched with good SATs and GCSE grades. This book is a practical guide on how to achieve this in your classroom and your school, based on our own experiences in various settings.

Why pick some when you can just have it all?

For all intents and purposes, the vision of the current school system is restricted to test scores, with a functional human being as a wholly accidental – and rare – by-product. In the largest (pre-COVID) health survey ever conducted on UK university students, one third reported having a 'serious personal, emotional, behavioural or mental health problem for which they felt they needed professional help'. More than 80% of these students reported that their symptoms began in secondary school.[9] In direct opposition to this, for most colleagues we have met, the vision is for happy and well-rounded human beings, with tests as a necessary evil which often just get in the way.

From the perspective of the traditional caricature, the political right wants authoritarian schools to produce quality assured machine parts which will serve to strengthen the national economy, whereas those on the political left are accused of wanting hippie heads to nurture happy and incompetent drifters whose sole ambition is 'exploring themselves' while cashing in on Universal Credit. (Although in these blurred times, no one quite knows their left from their right.)

---

9 Rethink, Largest Survey of Its Kind Reveals Extent of University Students' Struggles with Thoughts of Self-Harm, Loneliness and Anxiety (5 March 2019). Available at: https://www.rethink.org/news-and-stories/news/2019/mar/largest-survey-of-its-kind-reveals-extent-of-university-students-struggles-with-thoughts-of-self-harm-loneliness-and-anxiety.

Cooperative Learning negates the entire progressive vs. traditional dichotomy. In a Cooperative Learning classroom, the teacher is an authority who is responsible for teaching, setting the next learning path, structuring schemata and matching the learning to the needs of the learners. The learners, on the other hand, are responsible for learning – yielding confident, competent human beings with good test results in all phases. In the true spirit of collaboration, why not let everyone win, left and right?

Why it's not business as usual

The classic perception of businesses wanting docile factory fodder is no longer quite fair. Most of today's corporations hold the belief that schools should teach the most relevant and universally applicable skills, which reflect the demands of our complex, competitive, knowledge-based, technology-driven economy and society. This is why organisations such as Partnership for 21st Century Skills include brand names such as the Ford Motor Company, Microsoft and Lego.[10]

These sought-after skills include civic literacy, social justice awareness, ethical literacy, global and multicultural literacy and humanitarianism (to name but a few), and their promotion is mainly motivated by a belief that they will have significant consequences for our economy, democracy and society.[11] Try tick-box testing that.

> Employers have also called for the need to ensure that students develop effective communication skills, and the ability to talk for persuasive purposes has been linked to effective participation in civic and social life.
>
> **Bronwen Maxwell, Cathy Burnett, John Reidy, Ben Willis and Sean Demack,**
> *Oracy Curriculum, Culture and Assessment Toolkit*[12]

10 C. Fadel, *21st Century Skills: How Can You Prepare Students for the New Global Economy?* (Paris: Organisation for Economic Co-operation and Development/Centre for Educational Research and Innovation, 2008). Available at: https://www.oecd.org/site/educeri21st/40756908.pdf. See also https://www.battelleforkids.org/networks/p21.

11 Glossary of Education Reform, 21st Century Skills (25 August 2016). Available at: https://www.edglossary.org/21st-century-skills.

12 B. Maxwell, C. Burnett, J. Reidy, B. Willis and S. Demack, *Oracy Curriculum, Culture and Assessment Toolkit: Evaluation Report and Executive Summary* (London: Education Endowment Foundation, 2015), p. 7. Available at: http://shura.shu.ac.uk/10828/1/EEF%20Oracy%20School_21.pdf.

We assume that no one in business or government wants the national economy to fail or for youngsters to be jobless and disenfranchised. However, due to its age and size, the education system carries an incredible momentum and therefore the hope is always that (since it is impractical to tear it down and rebuild it from scratch) it can be somehow gradually upgraded. After all, what sane career politician would want to demolish an old factory and replace it with a garden if its fruits would be harvested outside of his tenure and may not even be quantifiable in any sense of the word?

Cooperative Learning presents a bottom-up solution to all the systemic issues that governments have neither the motive nor the means to address. It allows an educational paradigm shift to take place, one school at a time, without rocking the institutional super-tanker. Is the purpose of education to get learners to pass a test? Is it to serve business and fuel the economy? Is it for young people to lead rich and fulfilling lives? With Cooperative Learning there is no need to choose.

Chapter 1

What is Cooperative Learning? (And Especially What It Isn't)

It's the early 1980s in a suburb north of Copenhagen. Jakob is in the Danish equivalent of Year 6. He is sitting with five other children around a table: Madeline and Maria are discussing boys and trying out different types of make-up; Martin is throwing balls of crumpled paper at other groups of children, conveying messages that would be obscene if only he could spell; Andreas is reading a comic book; Jenny, who suffers from undiagnosed Asperger's, is quietly solving the task; Jakob is drawing a knight fighting a dragon in the margin of his textbook. When the bell rings, they all sign their names on Jenny's paper and the clueless teacher compliments them on their 'collaborative skills'.

So, first a definition: the Education Endowment Foundation describes collaborative learning as an approach which 'involves pupils working together on activities or learning tasks in a group small enough for everyone to participate on a collective task that has been clearly assigned. Pupils in the group may work on separate tasks contributing to a common overall outcome, or work together on a shared task.'[1]

> **Note:** *Cooperative Learning* and *collaborative learning* are used interchangeably in the Education Endowment Foundation's Teaching and Learning Toolkit to describe structured shared activities.

Collaborative or Cooperative Learning (used interchangeably in the Teaching and Learning Toolkit, but from this point on we will use Cooperative) is a term that refers to a number of such activities, which can stimulate thought and conversation about a given subject. The range and scope of said thoughts and conversations can (to a sufficient degree) be controlled, which means that Cooperative Learning can facilitate the full

---

1 Education Endowment Foundation, Collaborative Learning (13 November 2018), p. 1. Available at: https://educationendowmentfoundation.org.uk/evidence-summaries/teaching-learning-toolkit/collaborative-learning.

taxonomy spectrum from simple memorisation to analysis, debating and creating. The activities have simple steps that do not overwhelm learners; indeed, they help to focus minds on what needs to be learned.

The Education Endowment Foundation continue: 'Effective collaborative learning requires much more than just sitting pupils together and asking them to work in a group.' Or to put it even more directly: 'simple steps which focus discussion in an activity'.[2] This is the form of Cooperative Learning presented in this book: it pre-organises peer interaction into reusable patterns, which we have dubbed CLIPs. CLIP is an acronym for:

+ Cooperative

+ Learning

+ Interaction

+ Pattern

It is a *pattern*, in the sense that, again and again, it sequences your learners' *interaction* with your materials/tasks/questions and with each other, regardless of what or whom these might be in a given activity in a given lesson. But it's not just any interaction pattern; it's specifically a *Cooperative Learning Interaction Pattern*. Now, there are a number of definitions of what is required for a sequence of interactions to warrant the designation 'Cooperative Learning' as opposed to 'group work'. Here, we have chosen the leanest delineation by American educator Spencer Kagan, who first coined the mnemonic PIES.[3] PIES is an acronym for:

+ Positive interdependence

+ Individual accountability

+ Equal participation

+ Simultaneous interaction

This sounds a lot, but it is not,[4] because these four principles are always facilitated by the very pattern itself – no planning is required to achieve PIES.

---

2 Education Endowment Foundation, Collaborative Learning, p. 1.
3 S. Kagan, Staff Development and the Structural Approach to Cooperative Learning. In C. M Brody, N. Davidson and C. Cooper (eds), *Professional Development for Cooperative Learning: Issues and Approaches* (New York: Teachers College Press, 1998), pp. 103–123.
4 There are several other checklists of features required for Cooperative Learning, such as the five outlined by David Johnson and Roger Johnson, with whose work English teachers may be more familiar – see, for example, R. T. Johnson, D. W. Johnson and E. Holubec, *Cooperation in the Classroom*, rev. edn (Edina, MN: Interaction Book Co., 1991). Suffice to say, Cooperative Learning does a lot more than this, but this book is not an academic work: PIES is the baseline.

Let's investigate how PIES is facilitated using a CLIP called Catch1Partner, which is the centrepiece of this book. In the most basic form of Catch1Partner, each learner has a subject-relevant question on a card which they discuss in changing pairs (see Figure 2.1 for a step-by-step description).

> **Note:** Please do not over-focus on 'questions on cards'. These are just one example of many possible materials. As we will discuss in detail in Chapter 2, any physical object can be connected to any question across any subject – for example: worksheets (What do you have for question 3?), Numicons (Can you count out this for me?), photos (Was kannst du sehen?), graphs (What are the coordinates of this point?), rocks (How can you tell whether this is flint or not?) and so on.

Positive interdependence means that both children in each pair are needed to perform the CLIP and therefore both stand to benefit from their peer's successful outcome. They are not fighting for their teacher's attention, and nor are they competing to come up with the right answer first or even for their right to speak. On the contrary, the more one partner succeeds at his task, the more the other partner stands to benefit in the form of learning, and vice versa. This mutual reliance is embedded in all steps of the interaction. As children approach a potential partner, they might be requested to use phrases modelled by the teacher (in bold) – for example, '**Excuse me**, can I ask you a question, **please?**' 'Yes, **of course** you may' (smile, turn full body towards peer, establish eye contact, appropriate physical distance and voice volume – all modelled by the teacher). They take it in turns to answer each other's questions/solve each other's tasks and then swap cards and say, '**Thank you.**'

Usually (please be aware of the 'usually' here), this activity is used to remind children about something that has been taught previously (known in the current zeitgeist as 'activating prior knowledge' or 'revision'). However, all CLIPs can be used at any time and/or in any situation to facilitate many different objectives across a wide range of subjects – and social skills are not to be scoffed at. In the bigger scheme of things, an 80-year longitudinal study from Harvard reveals that the most essential quality in a good life is having good human relationships.[5] Other research notes that praise and positivity are social rewards,[6] and that social reward appears to use similar subcortical regions of the brain's reward system as receiving money.[7] The social element in these activities ties the process of learning to the stimulation of the brain's pleasure responses, which many children today find mainly in addictive games and social media.

The second aspect that defines Cooperative Learning, *individual accountability*, is the demand that both partners answer (how to ensure that they can answer and how to monitor this will be addressed throughout the book) and can do so using their own ideas and from their own unique understanding. A recent study showed increases in reward system activity during the answering of educational questions in conditions that favoured engagement and educational learning.[8]

Equal participation entails that both partners not only answer, but they have the same opportunity to speak from their own understanding and at their own length about the subject matter, irrespective of their different abilities. A key feature here is that lower-attaining children are just as important to the resolution of the CLIP steps as their higher-attaining peers. Indeed, the inclusion automatically afforded by Cooperative Learning is one of its many unique selling points. Obviously, some will talk for longer than others, but time is limited to the interaction of asking and answering the specific question, so at some point invariably they will both have answered, then swap materials and move on to the next partner. The truth is that verbose responses are the least of your problems; you will generally find yourself working to extend these conversations – which is where oracy gels into Cooperative Learning with a vengeance.

Finally, *simultaneous interaction* demands that everyone is doing all this at the same time – every single learner. There is no exception to this rule unless there are very specific special educational needs and disabilities (SEND) related reasons, and even so, any concessions should be temporary. For example, permission for an anxious child to remain in a corner and let people come to him should be seen as a step towards gathering the

5   Liz Mineo, Good Genes Are Nice, But Joy Is Better, *Harvard Gazette* (11 April 2017). Available at: https://news.harvard.edu/gazette/story/2017/04/over-nearly-80-years-harvard-study-has-been-showing-how-to-live-a-healthy-and-happy-life.
6   B. Dufrene, L. Lestremau and K. Zoder-Martell, Direct Behavioral Consultation: Effects on Teachers' Praise and Student Disruptive Behavior, *Psychology in the Schools*, 51(6) (2014): 567–580; and K. Sutherland, J. Wehby and S. Copeland, Effect of Varying Rates of Behavior-Specific Praise on the On-Task Behavior of Students with EBD, *Journal of Emotional and Behavioral Disorders*, 8(1) (2000): 2–8.
7   K. Izumo, D. Saito and N. Sadato, Processing of Social and Monetary Rewards in the Human Striatum, *Neuron*, 58(2) (2008): 284–294.
8   P. Howard-Jones, S. Varma, D. Ansari and B. Butterworth, The Principles and Practices of Educational Neuroscience: Commentary on Bowers, *Psychological Review*, 123(5) (2016): 620–627.

courage to mingle. Should you need reminding, you will find the PIES acronym explained in Appendix E.

Summary: For a classroom activity to warrant the noble label 'Cooperative Learning' it must pre-organise learner interactions into simple steps which combine to secure positive interdependence, individual accountability, equal participation and simultaneous interaction. If it does not, it is termed 'group work' – and the authors of this book wash their hands and then apply a good deal of sanitiser to boot.

Why is it so important to delineate Cooperative Learning?

An anecdote serves to answer this question. Some years ago, after much ado, Jakob finally got the opportunity to present Cooperative Learning to the leadership of a certain large primary school. He'd had this particular school in his sights for quite some time, having understood that the head teacher was decisive, open-minded, skilled and 100% dedicated to improving the lives of her children – basically, ready to take on Cooperative Learning. Full of confidence, Jakob arrived and did his song and dance; he explained the cost-efficiency, the benefits to teachers and children, the impact on the school's development targets and unique ethos, gave practical examples of activities, drew connections to the Sutton Trust's research on the pupil premium and even showed a short video. A few days later, he was informed by email that the school had zero interest – in a polite, roundabout British way, of course.

At the time of writing, that very same school is involved in a county-wide project where Jakob is responsible for the Cooperative Learning element. Its project leads, teachers and children are over the moon about the very activities he described in that original meeting. He was later given to understand that his presentation had been written off because the leadership felt they were already doing 'enough group work and talk partners'.

You might argue that talk partners is an interaction pattern, and on a very basic level it does appear to have some similarities. However, it does not support the equal participation required to meet the lofty standards of Cooperative Learning. Often, the voice of the loudest becomes the only voice heard. Moreover, the purpose of a real CLIP is to verbalise a thought process and not talk for the sake of talking. All opinions are not equal; some are a great deal more robust, sophisticated and well supported in terms of factual knowledge, logic and argument. But often those with good reasoning and understanding don't get their voices heard in the classroom. The equal participation enforced by CLIPs is a way of giving those thought processes a chance to be heard. Similarly, you will see that for the same reasons, talk partners does not secure individual accountability – much to the pleasure of any learner who yields the spotlight to their verbose mate because they cannot be bothered to engage in the learning.

The moral of this tale is that in order to understand what Cooperative Learning is, we must first define what it is not. As we've pointed out, Cooperative Learning is not group work or talk partners, and you will get the most out of this book if you work from this premise.

Cooperative Learning is not new. Let's pick an example of a CLIP from your halcyon PGCE days, from whence you will remember Think-Pair-Share. This classic CLIP, formalised by Frank Lyman back in 1981, is composed of three steps, *think*, *pair* and *share*.[9] Simply add a task, model and monitor, and – like all other CLIPs – Think-Pair-Share will work instantly in any subject and with any age group: 'What would you have done if you were a police officer and found Goldilocks breaking into the three bears' house?' 'Explain how you would solve this word problem from last year's SAT paper.' 'Summarise the impact of neoliberalism on the UK economy in the 2000s.' Think of a CLIP as a delivery tool (see Figure 1.1).

Think-Pair-Share is just one out of hundreds of CLIPs, many of which are used regularly by teachers all over the world without necessarily being called a Cooperative Learning Interaction Pattern or even Cooperative Learning. As one delegate said to Jakob after a training session: 'This is actually just really good teaching practice, isn't it?'

---

9   F. Lyman, The Responsive Classroom Discussion. In A. S. Anderson (ed.), *Mainstreaming Digest* (College Park, MD: University of Maryland College of Education, 1981), pp. 109–113.

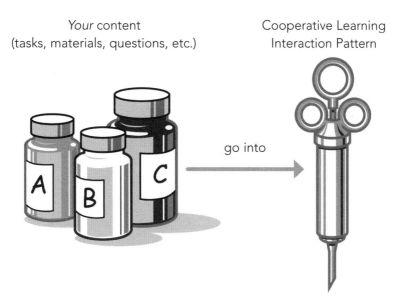

Your content
(tasks, materials, questions, etc.)

Cooperative Learning
Interaction Pattern

go into

Figure 1.1. Some teachers find it helpful to think of a CLIP as a delivery tool, in the same way that the same type of syringe may be used again and again to administer different medicines. Different activities with different objectives occur when your content changes. The steps in the CLIP, on the other hand, are immutable. You wouldn't throw out the plunger and think your syringe would still work. In the same way, you don't dump the 'pair' step in Think-Pair-Share.

The bigger picture

In fact, CLIPs can be used wherever you find a group of people, which would include classrooms, assemblies, study groups and even teacher–parent knees-ups – indeed, wherever something can be taught, learned, produced, processed or shared. For example, Jakob is currently developing Cooperative Learning to unpick extremely complex or toxic topics that involve multiple stakeholders, such as systemic racism in schools or unaligned mutual expectations between university students, tutors and leaders.[10] Indeed, many of the schools we work with use rough-and-ready CLIPs in staff meetings. If children can enjoy

10 J. Werdelin, In a Word: Co-Creative Conversation Explained, *cooperativelearning.works* (29 April 2019). Available at: https://cooperativelearning.works/2019/04/29/in-a-word-co-creative-conversation-explained.

them, why shouldn't adults benefit? Indeed, Drew's school, Stalham Academy, has successfully used CLIPs to get parents on board at parents' evenings.

Notwithstanding their instant and high impact, CLIPs such as Think-Pair-Share, once they have become routine (and only then), are simple to deploy in classrooms and give teachers a strong sense of effortless control and learners of all levels a sense of freedom and empowerment. (A side note here for readers interested in Cognitive Load Theory: the 'routine' element is important because research (and common sense) indicates that coordinating our communication and actions expends working memory,[11] potentially reducing the benefit of working together. Fortunately, the constant repetition of the immutable steps of the interaction pattern frees up working memory to focus on the task.)

As for materials, there is no need to buy new ones because CLIPs use your existing resources in more powerful ways, across all key stages and in all subjects. Nor do they throw out the baby or the bathwater: we have seen Cooperative Learning merge with existing good practice and support other approaches, invigorating and strengthening initiatives as varied as SOLO taxonomy, Philosophy for Children and Power Maths (see Chapter 9 for some examples).

Summary: A Cooperative Learning Interaction Pattern (CLIP) is a series of content-free action steps. These steps are pre-organised to support (if not directly enforce) PIES: positive interdependence, individual accountability, equal participation and simultaneous interaction. Once you mix the content – that is, your tasks, questions and materials – into the action steps of the CLIP, you have created an activity. For this reason, a CLIP may drive virtually any objective in any subject with any age group.

---

11 F. Kirschner, F. Paas and P. A. Kirschner, Task Complexity as a Driver for Collaborative Learning Efficiency: The Collective Working-Memory Effect, *Applied Cognitive Psychology*, 25(4) (2011), 615–624.

Evidence

Evidence about the benefits of Cooperative Learning has been found consistently for over 40 years in systematic reviews and meta-analyses of research studies, according to the Department for Education-backed Sutton Trust–Education Endowment Foundation Teaching and Learning Toolkit, and on average affords five months of additional progress per learner per year.[12] As we shall see in this book, Cooperative Learning seamlessly integrates other best practice strands in the Toolkit, including metacognition and feedback, which each yield a whopping average of seven to eight months of progress per learner per year, respectively.[13] As for Cooperative Learning's intimate connection with the research that underpins the 2019 Inspection Framework, we will deal with that shortly.

Knowing the path vs. walking the path

All this praise begs the question: if Cooperative Learning is truly the educational equivalent of a brand-new Tesla for the price of a 1999 diesel Toyota hatchback, why isn't everybody using it? Why doesn't every single primary and secondary school, college and university in the entire world just adopt Cooperative Learning? Why isn't every educational institution spitting out self-confident, competent masters of their own destinies, with top grades to boot?

One part of the answer lies precisely in the unhappy conflation of Cooperative Learning with disorganised group work which we noted previously. For example, there seems to be a tacit acceptance among teachers that any collaborative activity decreases the quality of individual assessment and requires you to run around keeping your charges on task. If this is the case in your school, you are not using Cooperative Learning in the specific form that we are recommending in this book.

Another part of the answer is the age-old maxim that the devil is in the detail. Poorly executed Cooperative Learning is possibly worse than regular unstructured group work

---

12 Education Endowment Foundation, Collaborative Learning.
13 Education Endowment Foundation, Metacognition and Self-Regulated Learning (30 August 2018). Available at: https://educationendowmentfoundation.org.uk/evidence-summaries/teaching-learning-toolkit/meta-cognition-and-self-regulation; and Education Endowment Foundation, Feedback (28 September 2018). Available at: https://educationendowmentfoundation.org.uk/evidence-summaries/teaching-learning-toolkit/feedback.

because it undermines the concept and turns teachers and children away from using it. Head teachers' fear of the Ofsted werewolf can lead to a too-desperate search for the silver bullet that will solve everything as if by magic. Following the regional schools commissioner's endorsement in 2016, Drew's school, Stalham Academy, had to issue a disclaimer email to schools whose staff were dispatched to witness the miracle. The upshot of that correspondence was that, while leaders and staff welcomed observers, under no circumstances would they accept responsibility for haphazard attempts to replicate 'Cooperative Learning' in other schools following a two-hour guided tour. This leads back to the fact that people hear and see what they want to hear and see. The visitors took what they thought was the key to Cooperative Learning, never checked their assumptions and thus missed the point. These ad hoc efforts to replicate Cooperative Learning are similar to the cargo cult phenomenon which is a classic bane of education: the forlorn hope that mechanical reproduction of a witnessed practice, without understanding or ownership, will somehow deliver the same results.

Make no mistake: Cooperative Learning *can* be a silver bullet and it *can* solve everything. However, what good is a bullet to someone who hasn't picked a target and doesn't know how to maintain and operate a firearm? Approximately the same use as a brand-new Tesla to someone who cannot drive and doesn't know where they want to go if they did.

This imperative to make decisions brings us to the final benefit we would like to point out in this introduction. Due to its step-by-step, hands-on nature, Cooperative Learning is possibly the world's cheapest, most non-threatening and effective professional development and coaching tool for teachers and school leaders alike. Because it is precisely that, a tool, you need to know what you want to do with it, and that entails investigating who you are and who you want to be as a teacher or leader.

Summary: Unlike group work, Cooperative Learning pre-organises learner interactions into a discrete set of action steps. These sets are called Cooperative Learning Interaction Patterns (or CLIPs) in this book. CLIPs define step by step how learners interact with materials and each other to achieve your various objectives and are pre-structured to enforce positive interdependence, individual accountability, equal participation and simultaneous interaction, while – as we shall soon see – making learning visible, reducing cognitive load and giving you full control of the teaching process. CLIPs allow the learners to focus on their learning and allow the teacher to monitor for misconceptions and plan teaching. It is the antithesis of the group work Jakob experienced as a child.

But what will Ofsted say?

Learning can be defined as an alteration in long-term memory. If nothing has altered in long-term memory, nothing has been learned. However, transfer to long-term memory depends on the rich processes described above. In order to develop understanding, pupils connect new knowledge with existing knowledge. Pupils also need to develop fluency and unconsciously apply their knowledge as skills. *This must not be reduced to, or confused with, simply memorising facts.* Inspectors will be alert to unnecessary or excessive attempts to simply prompt pupils to learn glossaries or long lists of disconnected facts.

Ofsted, *School Inspection Handbook*[14]

It would be remiss to overlook the impact that the Ofsted framework of September 2019 will have on schools in the coming years. The focus of the inspection criteria, its deep dives into curriculum subjects and its definition of learning have (at least) made schools consider and question the content and delivery of their curriculum.

This is not the place to debate the reasons or efficacy of the changes to the inspection criteria as it detracts from the main point; because Cooperative Learning is content-free, a change to the content matters little. As for its function as a delivery tool, Cooperative Learning can help to alter the long-term memory and allow learners to make links to other areas of the curriculum. And, depending on the contextualisation, modelling and relevant subtasks presented by the teacher, even closed questions can provide instant platforms for negotiating meanings and connections. (In that sense, Cooperative Learning is future-proofed against changes to curriculum.)

The very nature of judgement gives a hollow ring to the oft-repeated dictum, 'We shouldn't do it for Ofsted, we should do it for the learners.' Thankfully, the CLIPs don't 'do' anything for Ofsted; the research behind the effective teaching element of the new framework seems to welcome the use of CLIPs without further work on behalf of teachers. Indeed, the original draft Inspection Framework gives some useful insights into the rationale for the changes.

---

14 Ofsted, *School Inspection Handbook* (January 2019). Ref: 180041, p. 44; original emphasis. Available at: https://assets.publishing.service.gov.uk/government/uploads/system/uploads/attachment_data/file/801615/ Schools_draft_handbook_180119_archived.pdf. Note: this is a draft document that has since been archived.

The sequencing of learning has a very important role. A CLIP like Catch1Partner plays an equally important role by 'structuring elements [to] not only facilitate the memorising of information but allow[ing] pupils to understand it as an integrated whole'.[15] (We will see this in action in Ms Schmitt's German MFL class in Chapter 2, Activity 5.) Simply put, when there is specific information that needs to be reviewed, questions on a Catch1Partner card can stimulate recall in an organised and engaging manner. It allows the teacher to set the scene for the review and outline the transitions between different parts of the lesson. These elements can occur at different points in a lesson, or over a sequence of lessons, and can be integrated in different ways and at different times.[16]

For example, Drew observed Catch1Partner being used in a secondary history lesson, where the teacher started the lesson with some questions about prior learning on the Battle of Hastings. These included some basic link questions to what had gone before (e.g. 'Why was the Battle of Stamford Bridge important?', 'Why did William, Duke of Normandy, believe he was the rightful king?'). On a practical note, the teacher had clearly kept these cards from previous lessons and simply used the ones she wanted the children to recall. The students participated and returned to their tables (this was a high school where they sat in rows, not on islands of four). The teacher then presented the learning goal for the lesson (the role of the Catholic Church in William's invasion, posed as a question) and shared some knowledge (about two paragraphs) outlining the importance of the Pope's blessing, the papal ring and the instructions to the clergy in England to submit to William's rule. This was then followed by a separate Catch1Partner with specific questions going back over the information presented (e.g. 'Who was the Pope?', 'What is a papal bull'). Following that, the students returned to their desks and carried on with finding reasons (comprehension based) for the role of the Church at that point in history. This example shows how Catch1Partner can support the ideas laid out in Ofsted's overview of the research for effective teaching, dropped in at any point in the lesson for the reason of summary review, consolidation and the memorisation of information.

By using CLIPs with broad and varied questions (a mix of closed and open questions), combined with teacher talk on the academic content, the lesson structure thoroughly supported language. What was most striking, when viewed through the prism of Ofsted's research, was that the questions (which were well chosen, well worded and well thought-through) supported the students in talking to one another and verbalised their thinking

---

15 Ofsted, *Education Inspection Framework: Overview of Research* (January 2019). Ref: 180045, p. 14. Available at: https://assets.publishing.service.gov.uk/government/uploads/system/uploads/attachment_data/file/926364/Research_for_EIF_framework_100619__16_.pdf.

16 B. P. M. Creemers and L. Kyriakides, *The Dynamics of Educational Effectiveness: A Contribution to Policy, Practice and Theory in Contemporary Schools* (Abingdon: Routledge, 2008).

in a clear way. In the words of Ofsted: 'Questioning of pupils by the teacher, and of the teacher by pupils and by pupils of each other, can be used to check pupils' understanding and can help them clarify and verbalise their thinking.'[17]

To round off this chapter, we will refer to what Ofsted has to say about group activities, which supports our initial explanation in the Introduction: 'Group activities and paired work can contribute to learning, but to work together effectively pupils will require support, and tasks must be clearly structured.'[18] As should be clear by this point, the step-by-step activities, rigid staging and monitoring mean that Catch1Partner (and all other CLIPs for that matter) is a very structured way of giving learners the opportunity to verbalise their thinking and feel secure within a previously modelled subject area. As for the warning that 'group work requires both that pupils are sufficiently prepared, and that the activity is sufficiently structured',[19] we will discuss the importance of direct instruction and modelling in great detail.

The Ofsted research goes on to say:

Pupils need to be able to share, participate, listen and communicate, and tasks need to be structured so that every pupil has a clear and distinct role (to avoid 'free rider' effects). Pupils are therefore likely to benefit from explicit guidance on how to work collaboratively, from practising routines needed in effective groups and from having clearly assigned roles within a group work task. Teacher prompts and questions need to structure discussion, and active involvement is required to avoid misconceptions being reinforced. Group work should be carefully sequenced alongside other lessons and activities to ensure that pupils have sufficient prior knowledge.[20]

It would appear that even Ofsted can see a role for well-implemented CLIPs; they just haven't used the acronym CLIP.

....

17 Ofsted, *Education Inspection Framework*, p. 15.
18 Ofsted, *Education Inspection Framework*, p. 16.
19 Ofsted, *Education Inspection Framework*, p. 16.
20 Ofsted, *Education Inspection Framework*, p. 16. Note the copious body of research evidence quoted in
   support of this section.

Chapter 2

Catch 1 Partner –
an Exemplary CLIP

Effective collaborative learning requires much more than just sitting children together and asking them to work in a group; structured approaches with well-designed tasks lead to the greatest learning gains.

Education Endowment Foundation, 'Collaborative Learning'[1]

This chapter is akin to a recipe: a step-by-step guide to getting Cooperative Learning into your classroom and getting each stage right. There is no rush or specific timeline; when it comes to Cooperative Learning, quality trumps quantity every time.

To summarise, Cooperative Learning pre-organises how learners interact with each other and your chosen materials in a clearly delineated collection of action steps: 'OK, kids, do *this*, do *that*, then do *this*.' In Chapter 1, we mentioned Lyman's three-step Think-Pair-Share as one of the more well-known examples. There are many other such collections of action steps, each appropriate for different contexts and materials. What they all have in common is that they can be reused endlessly across all subjects and with any age group, and they always support positive interdependence, individual accountability, equal participation and simultaneous interaction. In this book, we term a collection of action steps a Cooperative Learning Interaction Pattern (CLIP).

This chapter – and, indeed, this whole book – is set up with practical classroom deployment in mind. We very strongly urge you to follow the recipe and make sure you and your learners master each basic activity before you move on to the next one.

---

1   Education Endowment Foundation, Collaborative Learning, p. 1.

The purpose of this chapter is to teach you how to use Catch1Partner, which has been a staple CLIP at Stalham Academy since the inception of Cooperative Learning in 2014. Once you have mastered its use in different contexts and with different materials and objectives, you will hopefully not only have engaged your learners and improved their results, but also achieved an understanding that will allow you to explore the other CLIPs described in Appendix A. Bear in mind though, as we have already noted, that although Cooperative Learning looks simple on paper, the devil is well and truly in the detail. While we hope that this meticulous exposition will help you to roll out Catch1Partner without major scratches to your ego or your classroom furniture, training and coaching at the hands of an experienced practitioner is not to be scoffed at.

In a sense, all the other chapters in this book act as commentary to this central chapter, and let you zoom in on specific areas, such as potential problems, where Cooperative Learning fits into the lesson and why, the role of the special educational needs coordinator (SENCO) or the wider context of the school. Of all these, we count Chapter 3 on direct instruction as the most important by far.

Why Catch1Partner?

Out of the six Cooperative Learning Interaction Patterns in Jakob's original training package to Stalham Academy, we have chosen Catch1Partner to give a detailed demonstration of Cooperative Learning because it is sufficiently simple and versatile to give any teacher or leader from EYFS through to Key Stage 5 an opportunity to get their feet wet without further ado. If your initial response is, 'What, I didn't get this book to learn just one thing,' bear with us. A Swiss Army knife is also 'one thing' until you pull out the tools. As stated above, mastery of the principles through experience is the key to success. Although you will see that Catch1Partner can facilitate a wide range of objectives, it is always better to do one thing with confidence and excellence than doing many things poorly. Do what works for you and your charges. When you are fully confident and you and your class can manage Catch1Partner in your sleep, feel free to begin testing the other CLIPs found in Appendix A.

What is Catch1Partner?

Bearing in mind that some of the other CLIPs are limited to very specific areas of learning and/or require a specific classroom setup, Catch1Partner is the ideal CLIP to get you started. It is simple to stage, requires no reorganisation of tables or seating arrangements, is highly adaptable and will quickly engage even the most timid learners.

In practice, learners mingle and ask and answer questions from various partners. Like most Cooperative Learning, it looks and sounds deceptively simple – 'deceptively' being the key word. You will discover in this chapter that Catch1Partner can be used to secure both formative and summative assessment and that it is excellent for training rapid recall and procedural skills, explaining knowledge, sharing and comparing understandings and ideas, presenting work or even for building and applying vocabulary and skills. From your perspective as a teacher, some benefits include the opportunity to monitor and check for understanding and to give precise, granulated feedback. Once the learners have tried Catch1Partner a couple of times, staging your activity may take you as little as seven seconds. Literally.

The task may take the form of flashcards with questions and answers or open questions, completed worksheets, images or objects (especially for EYFS) – basically, any materials that you would normally use in your day-to-day teaching and some you may never have even considered. Once the materials have been issued and the task presented, the learners execute the seven action steps of Catch1Partner:

1. Learners mingle quietly, holding up materials until they find a partner.
2. Partner A poses his/her question.
3. Partner B answers.
4. Partner A praises, thanks or helps.
5. Partners switch roles.
6. Partners swap materials.
7. Partners bid farewell and proceed from step 1.

As we said, deceptively simple. You can see these steps illustrated in Figure 2.1. At any time you need, you will find these steps in Appendix E.

1. Learners mingle quietly, holding up materials until they find a partner.

2. Partner A poses his/her question.

3. Partner B answers.

4. Partner A praises, thanks or helps.

5. Partners switch roles.

6. Partners swap materials.

7. Partners bid farewell and proceed from step 1.

Figure 2.1.The seven steps of Catch1Partner.

Using this guide effectively

Each of the following sections on activities explain how Catch1Partner will achieve one specific learning objective. Each section follows a roughly identical structure of seven subsections:

1. *Why are we doing this, Miss?* states the learning objective of the activity. Don't get confused: the same seven steps that constitute Catch1Partner may serve to generate wildly different outcomes.

2. Immediately after introducing the objective, the choice and best use of the relevant *materials* is then discussed.

3. *Staging your activity* gives practical examples of how to apply four basic rules to help you achieve this specific objective. By working your way through these varied examples, it is our hope that you will internalise and confidently apply these four rules when you go off and explore your own objectives with Cooperative Learning.

4. *Instruction-checking questions* is an element of staging so important that it warrants its own subsection. If you are not already familiar with the concept, you will find it useful in many other situations.

5/6. The subsections labelled *During the activity* and *After the activity* are reasonably self-explanatory and offer some helpful hints based on experience from a lot of classrooms.

7. The final subsection *When do I take the next step?* should be consulted before proceeding, as each activity builds skills (for teachers and learners) to support the next step. To be clear, until you can launch the activity in less than 10 seconds (excluding the time it takes to distribute the materials) and all the learners can execute the seven CLIP steps and specific task(s) with confidence and courtesy, do not move forward. Social skills is discussed specifically in the next section. Every single learner is responsible. Factor in everything, including banalities such as pushing chairs in to create more space to move about and prevent trips and falls (yes, safeguarding tick box!).

Getting off to a good start

This entire chapter – indeed, this whole book – is set up with practical classroom deployment in mind. We very strongly urge you to follow the recipe and make sure you and your learners master each basic activity before you move on to the next one. Slowly but surely is the name of the game. Again, we want to point out that Cooperative Learning does not remove the need for you to teach. (For more on this central tenet, please refer to Chapter 3.)

One good reason for not just rushing ahead is that these activities may well show you a completely new side to your learners, so you need to give yourself time to process these insights and decide how they can best be put to good use. If you have been running very front-loaded lessons, you may discover that the bright kids are not as bright as you thought they were, the introverts have a great deal more to say than anticipated, and the quiet, gentle and unproblematic girl who always sat still and listened to you attentively turns out to be a bullying hooligan.

Regardless, any difficulties that Cooperative Learning brings to light relating to personality, SEND issues, social skills or (in)appropriate vocabulary are all issues that you are required to deal with under the general statutory guidelines of your key stage in the various guises of character education; personal, social, health and economic (PSHE) education; spiritual, moral, social and cultural development (SMSC); social-emotional learning (SEL); fundamental British values; citizenship; and so on. Utterly irrespective of the promise that effective social and emotional learning will offer four months of additional progress,[2] respecting other people is a non-negotiable. On top of that comes the moral obligation that no matter what the formal test results, incompetence when it comes to human interaction has a greater negative impact on happiness in life than does incompetence in maths or English. If you have any doubt about this, try demonstrating your insight into inverse fractions or 'An Irish Airman Foresees His Death' the next time you have a conflict with your colleague or your partner.

On the bright side, if working with other people is a problem for some of your learners (and you want to follow recommendations 1 and 2 in the Education Endowment Foundation/Early Intervention Foundation Guidance Report on SEL[3]), you will find no

---

2   See M. V. Poortvliet, A. Clarke and J. Gross, *Improving Social and Emotional Learning in Primary Schools: Guidance Report* (London: Education Endowment Foundation and Early Intervention Foundation, 2019), p. 5. Available at: https://educationendowmentfoundation.org.uk/public/files/Publications/SEL/EEF_Social_ and_Emotional_Learning.pdf.

3   Poortvliet et al., *Improving Social and Emotional Learning in Primary Schools*, p. 1.

better tool to deal with this challenge than Cooperative Learning. Every day, in every lesson, in a tightly structured and controlled environment where they can hone the skills they ought to have, but often have not been taught at home.

Whatever your school values, here is a way to turn them from (often slightly smudged) wall decorations into a practical, lived, day-to-day reality. We will give practical examples from Stalham and other schools we have worked with as we proceed. Do not be put off: you will find that training social skills and subject knowledge go hand in hand, and that investing in the former will massively boost the latter.

Finally, Chapter 8 suggests solutions to some of the most common challenges for teachers who adopt Cooperative Learning.

Classroom control: the silence signal

Cooperative Learning presupposes that the learners communicate with each other, not you, for the duration of the CLIP. A consequence of this is that nobody will pay any attention to you. This is wonderful because it gives you the opportunity to quietly monitor the very visible learning process by listening in to the conversations between peers. However, it does present one challenge, which is to turn the attention of 30 ignited brains back to yourself. Virtually all primary schools have some system in place to secure attention, from salt shakers to clapping or whistling.

The following method is the one we recommend based on our experience, although as a primary teacher you should obviously do what works best in your situation. In spite of the fact that higher key stages stand to gain more from Cooperative Learning due to their larger vocabulary and more advanced communication skills, secondary schools seldom employ much in the way of organised peer learning. For secondary teachers worried about the transition between student-centred and teacher-centred learning, the silence signal is a useful tool.

The instructions to your learners are as follows:

When teacher lifts his hand:

1. Lift yours.
2. Be quiet.

3.   Where relevant, put down any pens.

4.   Look at the teacher and listen (and maybe gently help an inattentive friend to do the same).

The point is that nothing needs to be said. The silence spreads like wildfire across the room, and in a well-trained class you should be able to drop from full-on peer engagement to complete silence in approximately seven seconds. (A newly qualified teacher in North Norfolk claimed that her Year 4 class held the school record of four seconds, but if you aim for seven you should be fine.)

It is essential that you make your selected system for stopping an activity and bringing focus back to yourself an absolute non-negotiable. The time you invest in getting this to run smoothly will be won back by a factor of hundreds. If you neglect this crucial element, you will find yourself spending more time on getting control of the class than you will on teaching and learning. This comes back to social skills, which you will find have a very prominent place in these pages. Disrespecting the silence signal is to disrespect every single person in the room, including yourself. 'We don't punch people in the face. We don't dis-respect the silence signal.' Again: non-negotiable.

Catch1Partner with materials – step by step

To reiterate, Catch1Partner with materials is composed of seven steps:

1.   Learners mingle quietly, holding up materials until they find a partner.

2.   Partner A poses his/her question.

3.   Partner B answers.

4.   Partner A praises, thanks or helps.

5.   Partners switch roles.

6.   Partners swap materials.

7.   Partners bid farewell and proceed from step 1.

As a rule of thumb, these steps never change (with step 6 as a notable exception, which will be discussed where relevant). However, materials can be changed endlessly to match your class, your subject and the outcome(s) you want to achieve. Examples of relevant materials for each learning objective will be presented with each activity.

As you can see, Catch1Partner is not rocket science (really good teaching never is) and yet, along with its team-based equivalent Word-Round, it is a staple CLIP in every lesson at Stalham and is key to their incredible achievements with Cooperative Learning (discussed in Chapter 6).

Basic rules of staging an activity

There are four basic rules to staging an activity. Disregarding any one of these is the most common reason for landing in the disorganised muddle that is the very antithesis of Cooperative Learning. They are introduced here and you will also find them in Appendix E.

Rule 1: Scaffold the subject task

Cooperative Learning does not generate the intended outcomes in your lesson plan as if by magic. Cooperative Learning or not, if today's lesson is on converting decimals to fractions, you need to demonstrate step by step through worked examples exactly how this is done and make sure these examples and relevant subject-specific vocabulary are readily accessible (whether on the working wall, whiteboard or learners' materials). In this phase, you are their sage on the stage. Again, further details can be found in Chapter 3. The intention of scaffolding is that every participant has the support they need to contribute within the CLIP.

Rule 2: Be specific about what you want them to do

Be absolutely and utterly clear about what you want learner behaviour and interaction to look like, right down to when and how you want them to use specific phrases and vocabulary as they solve the tasks, especially in the early phases when freedom to move and speak in the class is a novelty.

Behaviour might include subtle listening skills, such as maintaining eye contact and nodding; or be purely practical, such as using an appropriate volume of voice (hint: this is one you want to stay on top of); or physical, such as maintaining a suitable distance from specific learners with autism spectrum disorder (ASD) or perhaps (minding any current health and safety guidelines) shaking hands, fist bumping, or similar when catching a new partner (step 1).

Interaction should cover how the learners are expected to work together on the subject task within the CLIP. For example, once learners pair up (step 1), partner A reads out his question (step 2) and waits for his partner to respond (step 3). But, given your experience with the low resilience of this particular class, you have made sure to remind learners of a specific phrase they must use if their partner draws a blank ('Maybe you could look at the example on the board?') or does not get it right ('Are you sure about that?'). The line between social skills and subject content is blurred because these two sentences might require a gentle smile as opposed to an exasperated sigh. Don't stop there: why not demonstrate 'least amount of help first' to arrive at the answer if partner B cannot get out of the muddle.[4]

> **Note:** Remember to use your general knowledge of your learners' capabilities and levels. As for subject-specific content, why make assumptions when Cooperative Learning gives you perfect opportunities for direct assessment? At any point in time you can have half the class explaining not only what they think the answer is, but also how they arrived at it.

Language might be subject specific (denominator, adjective, homonym, Iron Age, conductor), social skills specific ('Thank you!', 'When you don't look at me when I talk to you, I can't concentrate', 'Well done!'), metacognitive ('I know this because …', 'This makes me think of the previous lesson when I …', 'You got the answer right, but how do you know?') or be relevant for a stretch task ('What else can you tell me about this?').

Only you have the insight into your class, your materials and your objectives to make these choices. Give yourself time to reflect on how to stage the Catch1Partner to (a) get as much out of every second for every learner and (b) make each activity as much of a success as possible for as many learners as possible. In other words, you are scaffolding social skills in the same way that you would scaffold subject content.

---

4   See J. Sharples, R. Webster and P. Blatchford, *Making Best Use of Teaching Assistants: Guidance Report* (London: Education Endowment Foundation, 2015), p. 15. Available at: https://educationendowmentfoundation.org.uk/public/files/Publications/Teaching_Assistants/TA_Guidance_Report_MakingBestUseOfTeachingAssistants-Printable.pdf.

Rule 3: Show, don't tell

Don't just read out the above as a script: 'If [your partner doesn't know the answer] then [tell him to …]'. Rivet the kids with a proper Punch and Judy show where you model everything (with a TA if you are lucky enough to have one): how to find a partner silently, how to join up, how to smile, how to make eye contact, how to help, how to guide, how to thank, how to praise. And always model the mistakes you suspect your learners are likely to make based on your experience. You can even model the appropriate response to an inattentive partner (i.e. a response that does not involve the usual swearing or hitting or, worse, accepting being ignored by a peer in a learning situation). When you get to the point where you want to explore the team-based activities found in Appendix A, use a team to demonstrate to the class.

If you do not have another adult in the room, you can use a learner to demonstrate, but pick him or her wisely. The last thing you want is to waste time on prompting some deer in the headlights or spreading confusion because you selected someone whose sole joy in life is taking the mick. A smooth demonstration is especially crucial the first few times you are running the activity or whenever you add new subtasks or new vocabulary.

> **Note:** A subtask is any extra task you ask the learners to do aside from the core task embedded in the CLIP. For example, 'After your partner has answered the question about fractions on your flashcard, ask him or her to give you an equivalent fraction.' In every case, simple subtasks in the form of a fixed question – such as, 'What else do you know?', 'Prove it to me!', 'How do you know?' – do wonders to extend even closed questions.

Rule 4: Ask instruction-checking questions

This is a concept familiar to old Cambridge Certificate in English Language Teaching to Adults trainees. You basically turn your instructions into questions and ask the learners you pick out (not the ones with their hands up) to ensure everyone got it. If you noticed that a learner was staring out of the window, ask him. After a couple of times of the whole class staring at the same culprit in irritation because they cannot get started on 'the game' as he has to take three wild guesses before he admits to not having a clue, he usually does start listening. You could also target learners that you have noted have a specific issue: 'Amy and Stella, do we join up only with girls, or boys *and* girls?'

On the subject of leading questions, other examples might be: 'Johnny, are you going to shout out to your best mate from across the room and ignore the free person standing right next to you?' or subject specific: 'Ahmed, which words are we going to use to describe the shape?' or related to social skills: 'Izzy, what do we say to our partner when we are done?' There is no fixed recipe. You need to pick your instruction-checking questions based on the mood and make-up of your class, the complexity of your chosen task(s), the needs of specific learners and so on. Again, Cooperative Learning is not a straitjacket. It is a tool – although a powerful one.

Here we go.

Activity 1: Class-building (and introducing Catch1Partner to your class)

At a glance: Learners (and teachers) get to grips with the basic steps of Catch1Partner using cards with non-threatening social cues.

You are now ready to set up your first Catch1Partner. In the checklist in Appendix C, you will see a tick box entitled, 'Is the subject content relatively simple the first couple of times the CLIP is deployed?' Half of all the trouble when getting started with Cooperative Learning comes from underestimating the chaotic complexity unleashed by simultaneously engaging 30+ learners whose brains are not fully developed. We noted before that with Cooperative Learning, quality trumps quantity every time. It is important that you take small, steady steps where you feel you are in control, rather than barging ahead and doing everything at once.

Figure 2.2. Avoid making the first couple of Cooperative Learning activities too challenging.

Why are we doing this, Miss?

The objective is for the class to successfully execute the seven steps of Catch1Partner under their own steam for a couple of minutes. Start small, start simple. The best way to start small and simple is with a non-threatening, generic, class-building/icebreaker activity which allows you to assess the social skills you will need to inculcate if you want to get the most out of Cooperative Learning (and to help your learners to achieve well in real life beyond school).

Materials

All you need to get started is one icebreaker flashcard for every learner in your class and one extra for any adult in the room besides yourself. The reason you don't get one is that it is advisable to have at least one adult free to stay aloof and just monitor, so don't get involved if you are the only grown-up present, especially in the initial phase when you are introducing the CLIP. You will find a set of class-building flashcards in Appendix B (along with a link to a downloadable PDF version). The set is intended as a suggestion only, so please make sure to go over it and check that it is appropriate to your cohort. You will also find a template document you can download and fill in yourself, which might make producing and storing your own cards easier. Or just hit Google and find endless resources.

If you are working with non-readers, one thing that works well for initial social skills building is for pupils to bring a favourite toy or other item of importance for a Cooperative Learning show & tell (e.g. 'This is Bronson the Bear. I've had him since I was little. He has different eyes because one fell out, and my Mum had to put in another one. What's your dinosaur's name?'). Remember to model this engagement as you would in any other case, pointing out things they could mention if they get stuck, such as pointing out the colour, its texture, etc.

Staging your activity

Ask yourself: how would I like my ideal pair to engage from start to finish? (Also talk to your TA or other support staff where relevant, such as the SENCO.) Be as specific as you can – perhaps write it down. (You might like to have a look at the support materials in Appendix D, which may provide some formal structure for your planning.) The clarity of purpose required is what makes Cooperative Learning such an ideal professional development tool. In a nutshell, through the need to make decisions, you become aware of your choices, your vision, your skills, your strengths and your weaknesses as a teacher. Happily, Cooperative Learning also provides an ideal tool to deal with those challenges.

If you'd like a hint, our experience suggests that listening skills is the first area on which to focus. Make sure the learners know that they should actually look at the person to whom they have just asked a personal question. A second area of focus is the tendency for learners to gravitate towards their mates, or – especially in Key Stage 2 – to strenuously avoid members of the opposite sex. Both are detrimental to class cohesion and both are excellent starting points for introducing the obvious connection between Cooperative Learning and the ubiquitous school value of respect. So, in compliance with Rule 2 (Be specific about what you want them to do), when you model the activity in front of the learners, you might want to enact a negative example by looking out the window with a bored expression on your face, while your TA tries to engage you until she has to turn to the class and ask them what she should do about your disrespectful behaviour. You can be sure that answers will be forthcoming if you are sufficiently naughty. In the later key stages, we suggest a more conversational approach to social skills.

It's always useful to get consensus from the class on which behaviours are not acceptable, even if it is by asking if anyone disagrees. If no one puts their hand up, you can always refer back to this when there is an issue: 'Brian, you agreed that this was not acceptable, so why are you doing it now?' You could possibly elicit a couple of peer-to-peer responses to such behaviour on the board. Discuss (briefly) how we can show other people we are listening and perhaps take the opportunity to share how it makes us feel when no one pays attention to us: 'Is this how we want to feel in our class?' Then redo your modelling to demonstrate these new insights. Again, make decisions on how much time you should be spending on this; talking about something is not nearly as effective as doing it.

It is key that your school's behaviour policy is promoted in CLIPs to provide a sense of integration. Cooperative Learning is not a holiday from school rules, but their very embodiment: we do not accept bullying, ignoring, interrupting, teasing, pushing, off-task behaviour and so on. You will see in Chapter 6 that behaviour policies figure prominently.

> Cooperative Learning is not a holiday from school rules, but their very embodiment.

Instruction-checking questions

Below are some sample instruction-checking questions that you might want to ask after you have modelled the activity. (Remember, no hands up: just pick a learner by name and ask them. Let them answer and consider repeating the correct answer back to them.)

+ 'What material are you going to take from your desk, Peter?' ('That's right, Peter, your flashcards!')

+ 'When are you going to pair up, Hamida?' ('Right, Hamida, when you and your partner are finished, say goodbye, and both spot another free learner and pair with them.')

+ 'Bob, how do we show we are free?' ('Yes, Bob, we hold our card up high above our heads.')

+ 'Olivia, are you going to pair with your best friend or the closest person?' ('Closest, right – well said, Olivia!')

+ 'Alfred, are you going to form groups of three? Four? Five?' ('No, only pairs! Thanks, Alfred!')

- 'Is it OK for you to interrupt a pair before they are done, Dominic?' ('No, of course not!')

- 'What is your response to your partner, Chung-Hee?' ('Yes, we say, "Thank you for sharing that with me!" Perfect, Chung-Hee, thanks!')

- 'Siobhan, what will you do when you and your partner are done and have swapped cards?' ('Yes, that's right, Siobhan, you are going to hold your card up high above your head and immediately join up with a new partner.')

With regard to the first question, it is crucial that you never let learners leave their tables without the materials needed to complete the activity. Simply ask everyone to hold any relevant materials above their heads just before you set them off and do not start until you have confirmed that everyone is ready. Otherwise, you will need to deal with the missing card during the activity when you have other priorities. As always, it's seldom a good idea to pass out materials before you have given all your instructions. Unhappily, most teachers find that virtually any object in the room is more exciting than them, especially in the early key stages.

During the activity

Of all the strands in the Education Endowment Foundation Toolkit, feedback comes in at the top with eight months of progress per learner per year.[5] Feedback is only as good as the insight into learning on which it is based; therefore, give priority to monitoring what is going on during activities. Listening to learners' discussions not only often discloses what they know, but also the context of what they know and how they arrived there.

You can choose to partake in the role of a learner, but, again, our advice is that you should always have one adult responsible for the overall monitoring of behaviour and interaction. Check how your foresight on social skills and phrases worked (and didn't work) and what should be done instead.

---

5 Education Endowment Foundation, Feedback.

Figure 2.3. During activities, try to resist the urge to intervene; monitor instead.

Resist the temptation to intervene every time you see someone struggling; instead, give the pair a chance to flesh out a solution together. In the subject-oriented activities that follow, especially, where the materials hold the answer and/or the solution has been modelled and is available as a worked example on the learning wall or whiteboard, learners in the Cooperative Learning classroom should be expected to show resilience and responsibility.

However, any type of off-task behaviour or disregard for instructions must be relentlessly challenged. Not saying thank you, not swapping cards, dodging the closest free person, avoiding participation, bunching up in groups of three or more (unless teacher sanctioned for specific reasons, such as irregular numbers of learners or SEND-related peer support); all of these things are a direct threat to such lofty aspirations as class cohesion, peer self-confidence and the effectiveness of the lesson. Again, Cooperative Learning is not a lazy teacher doctrine.[6]

Note: Best practice is to position at least one adult where she can see everyone in the class to redirect as and when needed – for example: 'Sarah! Don't just walk past Justin.'

6 For more on the role of TAs in helping to keep things on track, please refer to the series of articles at: https://cooperativelearning.works/2017/12/14/making-best-use-of-tas-with-cooperative-learning-index-of-articles. The articles explore how Cooperative Learning supports the Education Endowment Foundation's seven recommendations which appear in Sharples et al.'s *Making Best Use of Teaching Assistants*.

After the activity

Should you choose to do a micro-plenary after an activity, it should serve a specific purpose. For instance, you might want to laud specific learners for following instructions well or going the extra mile to help, to share any good language you overheard or commendable behaviour you observed. You could also sample a couple of learners' experiences by asking if anyone wants to point out a helpful mate. If needed, point out anything you want the class to improve. Make the learners aware of any learning outcomes you observed during your monitoring too.

Remember, learners need to be trained to do Catch1Partner, just like everything else. If clarity is key to success, consistency is the very foundation. Keep refining this one simple activity. You can create superficial variations by using other sets of cards (e.g. jokes, trick questions, open questions specific to life in school, to family, to movies, to social skills, to morals). As for subject-related open questions, this is discussed in detail in Activity 3.

Remember, you don't need to stress if your card set does not have a different question for every learner in your class; you can have two or three flashcards with the same question. Drew and Jakob have observed that some classes often make use of as little as six questions in a regular class (i.e. repeating the same six questions on five cards to make 30 cards). It's more beneficial to encounter and discuss the same good question with perspectives from several different peers than discussing several superficial questions once.

A final note: you know the needs of your class and school ethos better than anyone. However, consider involving the learners in the reasons why you are introducing Cooperative Learning and get them involved in feedback: what went well? What didn't go so well? What could be done to improve it? Cooperative Learning should be more than a series of classroom activities. Rather, it should provide a mindset that matches the complexities of the 21st century beyond the smartphone: what do we need to do to successfully engage the human directly in front of us?

When do I take the next step?

You are ready to proceed to the next activity when you are able to stage this activity effectively, when you feel confident about doing so, when you remember to ask relevant instruction-checking questions to the right learners, and when the learners are able to execute the CLIP effectively on the prompt: 'Catch1Partner using the (X, Y, Z) flashcards. Hold them up above your heads! Ready? Go!' and terminate when you use the silence signal.

'Execute effectively' means pushing in chairs in accordance with health and safety procedures, proper behaviour, using appropriate language, holding cards high above their heads to signal they are looking for a new partner, voluntarily joining the closest available free peer, remembering to swap materials and responding to the silence signal within 7 to 10 seconds – the whole class being fully seated and at attention in less than 40 to 60 seconds (depending on key stage and room layout).

In some classes this takes a few days, in others a couple of weeks. In general, any doubts on your part as to whether your learners are capable of such challenging tasks as getting up from their seats without injury, holding a two-gramme card above their heads for no more than 30 seconds, communicating without shouting, paying attention to a single peer standing right in front of them for up to 90 seconds, and being quiet when instructed to do so, will mean they will doubt themselves too.

However, if children in 'the worst school in Norfolk' can, so can yours.[7] Do not underestimate your learners and, especially, do not underestimate yourself as a teacher. Cooperative Learning is a tool, and as powerful as it is, it needs a brilliant teacher such as yourself to wield it. Trust yourself, realise you are on a learning journey, proceed slowly but steadily and have a laugh with your learners when it goes pear-shaped – because it will. If you accept that to err is human and growing is a part of professional life, there is almost no limit to what Cooperative Learning will do for you.

Hence the next activity, which demonstrates how Catch1Partner can be used to facilitate rapid recall.

Activity 2: Rapid recall as entertainment

At a glance: Use Catch1Partner to drill facts, dates, vocabulary, concept definitions, number bonds and even simple procedures with instant confirmation or correction (known by Ofsted as making 'changes to long-term memory').

Although most would consider rapid recall to be in rather stark contrast to the preceding social activity, the steps of the CLIP remain exactly the same. The utterly different outcomes are generated only through the variation of the materials you put in and the

---

7   Incidentally, at the time of writing, the estate-based Henderson Green Primary Academy, aka the worst school in Norfolk, achieved 90% reading, writing and maths (combined) after two years of dedicated Cooperative Learning. There is more on Henderson in Chapter 6.

instructions you give. One of the many benefits of using CLIPs is that, despite all the bells and whistles of changing materials and tasks, they remain constant and recognisable to every teacher and learner in the school. This, in itself, is reason enough to prefer the organised, steady rollout of a CLIP with progressive expansion of objectives and variations, rather than trying to do everything at once. It is also a weighty reason indeed for MATs looking for non-invasive consistency across multiple sites to adopt Cooperative Learning (see 'What's in it for the multi-academy trust' in Chapter 5).

Note: As you shift the focus between fun class-building, rapid recall, peer assessment and metacognition, there are no recognisable changes to the steps of the CLIP: everyone grabs their cards, finds a partner, both ask and answer and so on. All the rules of good behaviour, signalling availability, volume of voice, thanking and praising are all relentlessly enforced.

Often associated with drilling or rote learning, rapid recall has an ominous ring to many teachers, and concerns were certainly not alleviated by recall figuring prominently in the new national curriculum and, more recently, in Ofsted's 2019 draft framework which defined learning as 'an alteration in long-term memory'.[8]

However, rapid recall simply means the ability to instantly and correctly draw out information from long-term memory. Maths teachers will recognise obvious examples (e.g. 2 + 2 = 4, sequences such as 1, 2, 3, or facts such as pi = 3.14 …). Yet, rapid recall of no-nonsense facts is relevant in all subjects: the conjugation of *faire* in French, key dates (or Henry VIII's number of wives) in history, the definition of 'conductor' in science or the word class 'adjective' in English. Not being able to remember such facts will require the learner to reinvent the wheel at every turn ('What was 2 + 2 again? OK, fingers out, let's start counting …') or resort to endless and time-consuming referencing of notes.

Jakob's grandfather told him that when he was in school (in the 1920s), they would memorise endless rhymes of each city and town along the main roads across Denmark. He could still remember them at the age of 80 and was disgusted that Jakob and his contemporaries could barely point to Copenhagen on a map, because they were taught to 'think for themselves'. Many years later, bitter experience and research into cognitive processes has proved his point. Rapid recall is necessary not only to achieve a reasonable speed when engaging in more complex undertakings, but is also a prerequisite for any form of creative

---

8   Ofsted, *School Inspection Handbook*, p. 44.

thinking because it leaves most of the working memory free to focus on higher level tasks: 'to develop fluency and unconsciously apply their knowledge as skills' as Ofsted further elaborates.[9] In Chapter 4, you will find this process explained from an adult's perspective – namely the process of learning to drive a car.

Jakob's grandfather did get one thing wrong, though: drilling need not be the sing-song of nursery rhymes, although it could be – that is dependent on the teacher, their musical and creative abilities and the culture within the school. Regardless, Catch1Partner provides an inclusive, entertaining and highly effective way to train rapid recall with endless opportunities to connect to context, complex thinking and metacognition. Phrased differently, Catch1Partner camouflages brutal and repetitive but necessary rote learning in the excitement of ostensibly child-centred interaction and movement to let your learners move into the realm of higher-level thinking.

Why are we doing this, Miss?

The main objective is to promote the rapid recall of general and specific subject-relevant content. This activity should be used in lessons without fail until the concepts and procedures you want your learners to master are fully memorised. It should also be used regularly to review knowledge and skills. (For more on reviewing, please refer to Chapter 3.) The secondary objective is to learn to ask for hints, give hints, ask for and provide examples or relevant procedures, congratulate, thank and praise.

Note: Given Ofsted's definition of learning as 'an alteration in long-term memory',[10] the snappy Catch1Partner is an ideal tool for spaced retrieval practice. Research has revealed that the key to successful learning via retrieval is not so much how much time is spent on learning, but how that time is distributed. Spaced retrieval practice is simply defined as arranging a given period devoted to learning into multiple sessions that are spread over time.[11] Simply drop in a Catch1Partner for five minutes every morning covering the current items you want moved to long-term memory. You will find some concise PDF booklets on retrieval and spaced retrieval at: www.retrievalpractice.org/library.

---

9   Ofsted, *School Inspection Handbook*, p. 44.
10 Ofsted, *School Inspection Handbook*, p. 44.
11 S. K. Carpenter and P. K. Agarwal, *How to Use Spaced Retrieval Practice to Boost Learning* (Ames, IA: Iowa State University, 2020). Available at: http://pdf.retrievalpractice.org/SpacingGuide.pdf.

Materials

Closed questions provide the exactitude that is the foundation for higher-level thinking.[12] In Cooperative Learning, closed questions have the added benefit of limiting the number of misconceptions that can be spread between peers. For rapid recall, only use flashcard-type materials with a question on one side and the answer on the other. Figure 2.4 shows some free online resources by Collins.[13]

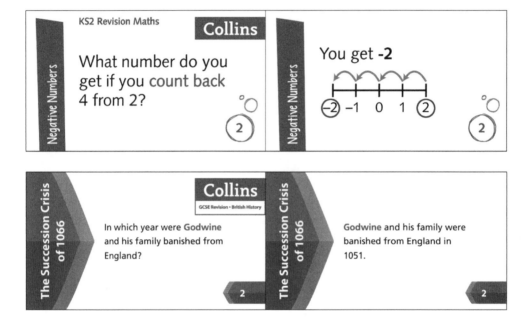

Figure 2.4. Key Stage 2 maths and GCSE history flashcards.

Training definitions is the classic and most obvious use of flashcards, such as a science teacher putting 'conductor' on one side of the card and 'A material that allows electric charge to move through it as an electric current' on the other. But flashcards also present an opportunity to drill simple procedures, which work in the same way as definitions; in maths, finding number bonds springs to mind. In German, you could have: 'Turn the

12 J. Werdelin, Cooperative Learning; Closed Questions, Closed Achievement Gaps, *cooperativelearning.works* (26 May 2017). Available at: https://cooperativelearning.works/2017/05/26/cooperative-learning-closed-questions-closed-achievement-gaps.

13 See https://collins.co.uk/pages/revision-collins-ks1-ks2-revision-and-practice-flashcards-resources and https://collins.co.uk/pages/revision-gcse-ages-14-16-collins-gcse-revision-and-practice-flashcards.

regular verb *bezahlen* into the past tense' on one side and the answer with a reminder of the procedure on the other (see Figure 2.5).

Instruction: Print and cut the learning cards of the bezahlen. Then place the individual cards for several verbs on a pile and mix. Now the cards can be drawn. The information on the cards must be read in memory. To match your solution, use the information on the learning sheets.

regular · haben · inseparable

bezahlen
(pay, ...)

Basic forms

bezahlt
bezahlte
hat bezahlt

Figure 2.5. Example of German verb flashcard.[14]

In this German MFL example, the crucial importance of direct instruction from the teacher, as we have outlined previously, should be crystal clear. Simple memorisation by ongoing review is one thing – and an effective one. But if the teacher wants students to master a general rule (e.g. the specific form of the past participle if the verb contains an inseparable prefix such as *be-*), a successful Catch1Partner requires that you have furnished them with a clear definition of inseparable prefixes and several worked examples where the procedure is applied, all the while verbalising your thinking process. This is a prime example of the connection between Cooperative Learning and direct instruction (as clarified in Chapter 3). German teachers will find a detailed description of a complex grammar lesson in Activity 5 (see page 69).

You will find an endless repository of suitable materials online – just Google 'flashcards', your key stage and the specific area you want to teach. Some are ready-made, others will need a bit of tweaking or some additions. Don't be afraid of tailoring materials to suit your needs. Again, you know best your class and your objectives.

---

14 See https://www.verbformen.com/conjugation/worksheets-exercises/lernkarten/bezahlen.pdf. The full set, produced by Netzverb under a Creative Commons licence, includes simple present, simple past, imperative, present subjunctive, past subjunctive, participles and infinitives.

Staging your activity

To demonstrate the staging of this first rapid recall activity, we will use simple multiplication from times tables.[15] Looking back at Rule 1 (Scaffold the subject task), you will need to recap what the learners already know about the relevant times table, and especially to remind them about any strategies you might have taught them to solve multiplication with the least amount of work. Why not train methods and mental arithmetic simultaneously with the memorisation?

As for Rules 2 and 3 (Be specific about what you want them to do/Show, don't tell) be specific about the interaction and language you are expecting the learners to use, so that you maximise the return on your investment in time, in and out of class. For example, model what learners should do if their partner gets it wrong or becomes stuck. Base your demonstration on things you are expecting to happen from your previous experience. Always remember that Cooperative Learning does not change *what* you teach, but *how* you teach it, so apply some *savoir faire*. As you should be reviewing the same card sets regularly, you can tinker with the details of the interaction until you get everything the way you want it.

Instruction-checking questions

As for Rule 4, asking the usual instruction-checking questions is vital. At this point, most learners should be able to move around the class quietly, using their materials to signal when they are free, pairing up with the closest person (regardless of gender and social standing) and similar basics. The challenges will most likely revolve around details of hinting, supporting, encouraging, praising, thanking and, for some learners, discussing and negotiating appropriately. Make no mistake: this needs to be modelled. You cannot count on learners just knowing such complex and vital life skills from home, no matter their social background.

Some instruction-checking questions for this activity include:

+ 'If our partner doesn't know, should we just turn over the card and show him the answer, or do we prompt him?' ('That's right, we prompt him!')

+ 'So, what can we do to prompt him?' ('Brilliant! We can refer to the examples on the board or even give an example of our own, like I just did with Paisley in the demonstration.')

---

15 A sample flashcard is available at: https://drive.google.com/drive/folders/1aqfQGiV7VLEMF2NoivlwtUdk1 Xe-0uu2 (https://bit.ly/TheBeginnersGuideDownloads).

+ 'If we disagree with our partner's response, do we just show her the answer, swap cards and carry on to the next partner, or do we explore the disagreement with her?' ('Yes, we explore the disagreement.')

+ 'And how can we politely say that we disagree?'

And so on. You know your learners and you know what their challenges are.

During the activity

If you've spent sufficient time on the previous activity, basic interactions and behaviour should be ticking along nicely and you should now be able to focus on monitoring and assessing subject knowledge. 'Visible learning' has become a bit of a buzzword thanks to John Hattie. By making learners present their thinking and negotiate their understanding orally, Cooperative Learning automatically provides more visible learning than you can reasonably cope with.[16] Therefore, make sure you distribute your attention. If you have one, make good use of your TA to support you in this.

Listen and interject only when needed and prompt only if the learners are completely stuck. Model the sentences and phrases you wish to hear. The question that always arises is to what degree you should intervene when you see learners struggling. Again, take a step back and draw a deep breath. If you have scaffolded language and modelled the activity appropriately, there should be no excuse for learners being unable to carry out the task. If intervention is strictly necessary, try to limit yourself to as few words as possible: 'Look at the learning wall!', 'What could you say now, Thomas?', 'Yes, you could say … as I did in the modelling. Try that.'

What you are really looking for are any pervasive problems that scupper the success of your activity. If you see a recurring theme as you monitor – perhaps you realise that you overlooked something when you presented the concept(s) or made a wrong assumption about their prior knowledge – address this immediately with the whole class. Signal 'Stop' (we recommend using the silence signal, as previously discussed) and, in a few crisp sentences, say what needs to be said to address the issue. Then set them off again. The point of making learning visible is that you can step in and give feedback on the fly. Ideally, you want the time between you identifying a problem, challenging it and resuming the activity to be as short as possible, so this is where classroom management really becomes important. For any learner to disregard the silence signal (or your school's equivalent) is tantamount to bringing drugs into the school and should be dealt with promptly and

---

16 There is more on this in the section on SOLO taxonomy in Chapter 9.

appropriately. As you will see in Chapter 6, Drew's school had clear responses to ignoring behaviours for learning.

After the activity

As always, consider whether or not it is worth your while to do a post-activity plenary. If your objective was to train procedures or drill rapid recall, and the learners did this successfully, what is there to talk about? On the other hand, if your objective was to assess their abilities in order to drive forward the teaching of, for example, the specific procedures required for multiplication, and monitoring revealed issues pertinent to that, then address it. In general, any lengthy or complex corrections should be relegated to plenaries, never within the activity itself. As for individuals' misunderstandings, your anonymous observations should enable you to correct specific learners without putting anyone in the public spotlight, whether it's a quick comment on the spot or later on in private.

Remember that Cooperative Learning is a brilliant assessment tool, but it is not a specialised test system. If you want to test the precise impact of your activities on each individual, do a baseline time-sensitive test on rapid recall of the tasks on your flashcards. Then do Catch1Partner at the start of every lesson for a period of time, redo the test and compare the results. You will be surprised.

> The substantial benefits of collaborative learning on later memory retention were demonstrated ... not only for the target subset, but also for semantically related information.
>
> Jacquelyn Cranney, Mihyun Ahn, Rachel McKinnon, Sue Morris and Kaaren Watts, 'The Testing Effect, Collaborative Learning, and Retrieval-Induced Facilitation in a Classroom Setting'[17]

When do I take the next step?

In addition to continued embedding and improving of the basic skills found in the class-building activity, learners must now learn to stay on task and strive to answer all the subject-specific questions they are presented with to the best of their ability. This will be

17 J. Cranney, M. Ahn, R. McKinnon, S. Morris and K. Watts, The Testing Effect, Collaborative Learning, and Retrieval-Induced Facilitation in a Classroom Setting, *European Journal of Cognitive Psychology*, 21(6) (2009), 919–940 at 938.

an ongoing struggle because it applies equally to any and all tasks in any Cooperative Learning activity much more so than in individual work. The impact of lacking focus is instant, and, just as in adult life (which school is supposed to prepare the learners for), always has consequences for others. Hence, the message must be clear: the failure to pull your own weight negatively affects other people, exactly as it does in the real world of family and professional life and in democratic society at large. Simply giving up is not an option.

On the other hand, every learner must know that there is help available, not only in the shape of adult input but also from their peers. This transition – from being a helpless child in a group of other helpless children waiting for guidance and support from grown-ups who are static reservoirs of infinite knowledge to being an empowered individual who bonds with other empowered individuals in a learning situation (including teachers) – is a crucial factor in shifting the burden of learning on to the learners, where it should be, leaving the teacher free to teach, which is likely the reason you entered the profession in the first place.

In summary, you are ready to move to the next activity when you are able to stage this activity confidently and effectively, and the interaction and behaviour needed is perfected sufficiently to let you monitor for subject learning more than for behaviour and interaction. Also, you should be consciously building your own sense of when and how to interject effectively during the activity, and when to stay aloof and let the kids apply themselves. Just remember that if you are the only adult in the classroom, you need to balance your overview of the class against the needs of any one individual.

It goes without saying that all learners must stay on task and strive to answer all questions to the best of their ability before asking to see the answer. They should ask partners for, and give, hints, and congratulate, thank and praise.

Summary

Hints on materials for rapid recall:

- Materials need not be fancy flashcards; you could just use previously marked worksheets, where the answer has been confirmed. With each new partner, they pick a task and check the answer. Alternatively, you could ask the learners to share a wrong answer and discuss (in every case, don't forget to model what such an engagement might look like).

- In general, flashcards should be in sets covering the same topic. If you are learning about volcanoes, for example, train specific vocabulary in one set: *lava, tectonic plate, ash, ash fall, igneous rock* and so on.

Some examples of front-of-card questions for Catch1Partner to facilitate subject knowledge (the answer goes on the back of the card):

- When did the First World War start? (cross-curricular)
- What is a factor? (maths)
- What is photosynthesis? (science)
- What is an autobiography? Give examples. (English)
- What is a cardinal number? (maths)
- What is an adverb? (English)

Some questions to critique your homemade flashcards:

- Is the language appropriate?
- Is the question clear?
- Is the answer clear?
- Why choose this particular question and not another one?
- What could be the difficulties for learners with this card?

Activity 3: Input processing through open questions

At a glance: Use Catch1Partner to prompt targeted, scaffolded discussions using virtually any material.

This version of Catch1Partner is a workhorse of Drew's Teaching and Learning Cycle, which is discussed in its proper context in Chapter 4. As we already know, there is no changing the seven steps of the CLIP, only the materials and tasks. What makes this activity simple to stage compared to the Q&A cards in the previous activity is that the materials used here provide only a question or prompt, but no answer. It is solely the task you set that delineates the range and scope of the partners' discussions. A science teacher could print off 30 animal images and, at various stages in primary, these could be used to attain a range of objectives from the science curriculum – for example: providing a simple description using subject vocabulary (*fur, scales, legs, horns, shell, hooves, claws*); comparing animals and examining recurring patterns; debating their likely habitats based on their characteristics; and, in the same vein, classifying them by diet, class, process of reproduction and so on. Essentially, the same materials can be used right up to Year 6, where learners should be discussing their 'reasons for classifying plants and animals based on specific characteristics'.[18] (So, it is good practice to laminate such pictures from day one.)

Ask students to explain what they have learned.

Barak Rosenshine, 'Principles of Instruction'[19]

This is, of course, where the astute reader recalls the classic critique of peer learning: in free, open discussions the children will teach each other the wrong things, and there is no way to stop them! Ironically, this is where Barak Rosenshine and direct instruction really prove their value. As we have made clear in this book, Cooperative Learning activities do not take place in a vacuum. Rather, they fit snugly into the specific stage of practice where the learner transitions from the teacher's instructions and worked examples to independent application. Think about it: CLIPs provide every learner simultaneously with opportunities for: unrushed, detailed discussions; sharing, comparing and checking their understanding of the teacher's instructions; applying vocabulary and skills; asking in-depth clarifying questions; and identifying and learning from mistakes. And all before they move on to any individual work. Catch1Partner is just a time-efficient way to get all learners to that point.

The upshot is that CLIPs are cushioned on all sides by the teacher's instructions, observations and feedback, and this is the best bulwark against learners going off on a tangent. It is therefore crucial that the task you set intimately reflects what you have just taught. The objective of the question-only task in Catch1Partner is not the endorphin rush of 'getting it right' that children obtain from the Q&A cards in the previous activity. The objective of the question-only card is the dialogue that hones understanding (this is the inner voice referred to in Chapter 4). And this dialogue must be directly based on teacher modelling (this is the direct instruction referred to in Chapter 3).

18 See https://www.gov.uk/government/publications/national-curriculum-in-england-science-programmes-of-study/national-curriculum-in-england-science-programmes-of-study.
19 Rosenshine, Principles of Instruction, 19.

CLIPs are cushioned on all sides by the teacher's instructions, observations and feedback, and this is your bulwark against them going off on a tangent.

As for the revision stage of a lesson, it logically requires that the materials to be revised have already been introduced and trained in one or more previous lesson(s). Ideally, you would use cards from yesterday's guided practice in today's revision task ('I remember this from yesterday! Mikey explained to me that …'). Use the same cards sets for weekly and monthly reviewing. We cannot overemphasise how important it is that you reuse materials as much as possible. If you want changes in long-term memory and integration into larger concepts, this revisiting of the same materials in multiple contexts over time is key.

Summary: At a loss for words? Replicate the same question on two cards, so instead of having to come up with 30 questions in a 30-strong class, you only need 15. So what if some learners see the same question multiple times in a session? In the vast majority of cases, they will be revising, explaining and discussing it with a different peer.

Why are we doing this, Miss?

Depending on the way you model the discussions and interactions between learners when you stage the activity, the range of ancillary objectives are virtually endless. They might include presenting a coherent counterargument in a disagreement, using parallel examples to explain your point or questioning techniques to pinpoint a specific issue within a larger problem that your partner is confused about. Any secondary school teacher who doubts the relevance of Cooperative Learning in the later key stages should consider very carefully the benefit of 15 pairs applying such skills across multiple subjects and in various situations on a daily basis from Year 7. The ability to communicate coherently is as important in maths and science as it is in English. Presenting at two separate Association for Science Education annual conferences with science oracy specialist Naomi Hennah and Ben Rogers, the author of *The Big Ideas in Physics and How to Teach Them*,[20] Jakob has demonstrated the power of CLIPs to support the reading of dense scientific texts to teachers in Key Stages 3 to 5.

---

20 B. Rogers, *The Big Ideas in Physics and How to Teach Them: Teaching Physics 11–18* (Abingdon and New York: Routledge, 2018).

Materials

Materials constitute cards or papers with any type of subject-relevant question, statement, graph, image and so on. Materials might also be physical objects: in science, you could give each learner a mineral sample or a dried plant. In one EYFS class, Jakob has seen the youngest children walking around with toys, describing their names and telling stories (this is one where you skip the swapping step in the CLIP or risk a crisis!) and slightly older children carrying objects of various shapes and colours, sharing their names and certain attributes based on teacher direct instruction ('Your object is a *cube*, it has six *faces* – what about mine?'). Regardless of materials, the task itself should facilitate discussion, investigation and explanation.

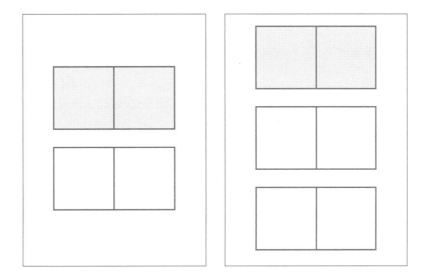

Figure 2.6. Fraction cards showing ²/₄ and ²/₆ respectively.

When you do use cards, remember that the preceding teacher instruction and modelling may dispense with the need for any written instructions on the materials themselves. In Figure 2.6, the simple drawings of fractions serve only as prompts, which leaves the teacher free to set up different tasks using the same cards simply by posing different questions. In Chapter 4, you will find a transcript of an actual dialogue between two children working with these two cards in response to the task: 'Identify the fraction and any equivalent fraction'. But the task might as well have been: 'Which one of us has the biggest fraction?'

Note: Subject-specific open questions that work in different contexts are a brilliant way to save preparation time (e.g. the flashcards for reading fiction/drama found in Appendix B). These generic reading comprehension questions are useful when learners need to discuss a book or play they are reading. Questions such as: 'Who is the main character in the story?', 'Do you like him/her? Why?' and 'Where does the story take place?', 'What is the place like?' all work equally well for Shakespeare's *Othello* and Neil Gaiman's *Coraline*.

Staging your activity

Rule 1 (Scaffold the subject task) is probably the most important element when making the transition from closed quiz-type questions with answers on the back of the cards to open questions where learners' thoughts can potentially wander off in any direction. Make sure there is ample support in the form of examples on the board where they can be easily referenced and carefully model your thinking process out loud. How crucial this scaffolding is really depends on the scope of the knowledge you want the learners to process: how precise is it, and how fuzzy can you allow the edges around it to become?

Make sure there is ample support in the form of examples on the board, where they can be easily referenced and carefully model your thinking process out loud.

For example, if you are posing open questions about *Romeo and Juliet*, of the type, 'Discuss whether family or love should come first, and why', you just need to make sure that each student has a reasonable grasp of what happens in the play. You might want to set up ground rules about always furnishing an explanation (never allow a bland 'yes' or 'no' to any question), whether you are expecting the partner to riposte with a critical question or embellish their partner's response with examples. On the whole, as long as they know the story and can put two words together, you should be OK.

This is less applicable when you start to look at the techniques used by an author. If your questions are more along the lines of, 'List and describe some of the literary devices in the opening of *Macbeth* and explain why you think they are/aren't effective', you had better provide examples of said devices before you set them off. While there might be a lot of valid opinions about whether a certain device is effective, there can be no variation in opinion about the definitions of alliteration, simile or metaphor. This basic factual knowledge has to be in place for meaningful free thinking and discussion to take place.

Unlike the *Romeo and Juliet* task, where learners discussed their personal attitudes to responsibility to family vs. falling in love, the *Macbeth* task operates within a predefined and agreed upon framework – that of literary devices. Students are not allowed to hold the opinion that a certain phrase is a poor simile when that phrase is actually a metaphor. (We note drily that if this relationship between facts and opinions had been taught more effectively to earlier generations, today's political climate might look very different indeed.)

In Rule 3 (Show, don't tell), you should model how peers are expected to ensure that they are discussing within the same framework: 'Andrej, a simile is not a metaphor because a metaphor is a statement that one thing is actually something else and that's not the case in this sentence. So, please do continue, why do you hold the opinion that this *simile* is ineffective?' In summary, if you want discussions to straddle both hard and soft outcomes, make sure the learners have the hard knowledge they need.

> Basic factual knowledge has to be in place for meaningful free thinking and discussion to take place.

Where the primary teaching objective is hard knowledge, pure and simple, and the point of any discussion is only to support memorising and applying that knowledge effectively to a range of situations, then Catch1Partner works in that situation too.

Let's say you are an English teacher who wants learners to skim paragraphs from various novels to identify instances of the passive voice. When it comes to grammar, you don't really want any personal opinions or fuzzy edges. This or that sentence either is or isn't in the passive voice, and learners need to describe how they know. In this scenario, it is crucial that you first show/remind the class how that specific grammatical structure works, provide some quick test tools, warn against common mistakes and so on – all the basic teaching you would do anyway. But, as for Rule 2 (Be specific about what you want them to do), you would model a specific thinking process with an assistant or carefully selected learner, while systematically applying any relevant subject vocabulary, as in the following:

(The learners' materials constitute a number of photocopies of paragraphs with a passive voice sentence from various books. In his modelling, the teacher is using an example from Douglas Adams' *The Restaurant at the End of the Universe*: 'The story so far: In the beginning the Universe was created. This had made a lot of people very angry and been widely regarded as a bad move,'[21] which he has projected onto the whiteboard, so the whole class can see him explaining the card to Annie.)

Teacher: OK, Annie, so, I'm skimming your paragraph, and this second sentence has got 'was' in it. So, I'm now checking to see if there is a verb ending in '-ed'. 'Be' can be an auxiliary verb and when 'was' or 'is' is followed by a verb ending in '-ed' that indicates a passive voice, and in the example we looked at before *[points to one of his many worked examples on the board]* the past participle is used in the passive voice. And there *is* an '-ed' ending, see: 'In the beginning the Universe was creat*ed*.' So that is a sentence in the passive voice. Am I right?

Annie: I totally agree – brilliantly done! Can you find any other indication this might be a passive voice?

Teacher: Well, there is another thing: we don't know from this sentence who created the universe, so that also makes me convinced it's in the passive voice. Do you agree?

Annie: Yes, that makes sense. But can you explain to me *[Annie looks at the whiteboard with examples of stretch tasks]* ... if you wanted to say who created the universe in this sentence ... like, how could you do that?

Teacher *[pretending to struggle]*: Uuuuh ...

Annie: Look at the example on the left – do you see that *[points to whiteboard]*?

Teacher: Right, so you add the person doing it at the end ...

Annie: Brilliant! Now, can you give me an example using my sentence: 'The universe was created ...'?

Teacher: The universe was created ... by ... *by a race of scientist aliens* ...?

Annie: Well done, thank you. Now it's my turn. Let me skim your paragraph, please ...

You can see how the teacher is meticulous about using subject vocabulary, such as 'auxiliary verb' and 'participle'. Annie has been prepared for her role in the modelling and her

21 D. Adams, *The Restaurant at the End of the Universe* (The Hitchhiker's Guide to the Galaxy series, vol. 2) (New York: Del Rey, 1995 [1980]), p. 1.

question, 'Can you find any other indication this might be a passive voice?' is a subtask and is listed as such on the whiteboard: it follows the main task and serves to extend the learning. 'Look at the example on the left – do you see that?' reminds learners to use the support offered by the worked examples, which are left on the board for this exact purpose. Her question, 'If you wanted to say who created the universe in this sentence ... how could you do that?' demonstrates to learners how to hint. Further enforce these points in the instruction-checking questions as needed.

Instruction-checking questions

As always, remind learners about any basic behaviour you have noticed that is beginning to slip ('Maria, do we run screaming and shouting and pushing across the room to interrupt our BFF and her current partner, or do we quietly walk up to the nearest free individual, even if that person is a boy?'). But when using materials with open questions, your instruction-checking questions should focus on giving concrete subject-related support. Here are some examples of instruction-checking questions (and their confirmations) about identifying passive voice sentences in a paragraph:

+ 'Vladislav, do we slowly read our partner's paragraph aloud, or do we skim it silently, looking for indicators that the passive voice is being used?' ('Yes, bingo! We skim it.')
+ 'When we skim our partner's paragraph, which are some of the indicators that a sentence might be in the passive voice, John?' ('Yes, the past participle is a good indicator!')
+ 'But, can we be sure a sentence is in the passive voice just because it contains the past participle, Jordan?' ('No, exactly, that's right, Jordan, we can't! As we saw in this comparison right here on the board [points to example].')
+ 'What verb must the past participle always follow to form the passive voice, Ying Yue?' ('Yes, a form of "be" such as "is" or "were": "The runaway *was captured*." Well done, Ying Yue!')
+ 'Can we always count on a participle ending in "-ed", Alek?' ('Bingo! Some verbs are irregular: "The runaway was *caught*." So be careful!')

And so on. When pondering instruction-checking questions about subject matter, ask questions about only what is vital in order for them to succeed with the task at hand and reduce answer options to yes/no or single-sentence responses, or you will find yourself spending so much time on learners waffling that the rest of the class will forget what they are supposed to be doing.

During the activity

You should continue to monitor for all the basics and intervene as described in the previous 'During the activity' sections. With open questions, the monitoring is more important than ever. As usual, are the learners on task? Are they referring to any relevant common framework? Are they correctly applying subject vocabulary? And, the killer, are they agreeing on something that is wrong? Continue to apply any good practice you have identified that works with this particular class. Always think of your knowledge as cumulative. Since the basic steps in a CLIP remain the same, there is an infinite series of opportunities to improve and refine its execution. As always, demand that your instructions and directions are rigorously followed.

> Since the basic steps in a CLIP remain the same, there is an infinite series of opportunities to improve and refine its execution.

After the activity

Because open questions open the door to misconceptions, it is a good idea to do a couple of checks. Pick random learners or ask a hinge question to be answered using mini whiteboards or hand signals – employ any technique that works for you. At Stalham, a Catch1Partner with open questions is usually followed by the in-team CLIP Word-Round (see Appendix A), where learners return to their teams of four and take timed turns describing/recapping/musing on their experiences during the Catch1Partner, usually based on whatever card they had in their hand when told to return to their seats. This means that each learner gets his new understanding rechecked by three people simultaneously and has the opportunity to ask questions. If a whole team disagrees, it's a sign there is a real misunderstanding that the teacher needs to unpick.

When do I take the next step?

Open questions with subject content and subject-oriented objectives (as opposed to the social games with which we started out and the Q&A cards with closed questions) are an acid test as to whether your learners can take responsibility for their learning. Discussions are open and hence potentially explorative, yet must take place inside a clearly delineated framework; a question about violence in *Macbeth* must not lead to a recap of escapades in a favourite first-person shooter game. 'Freedom with responsibility' is a concept of universal import and here is a good opportunity to explore its application.

The above three activities are generic workhorses, and many teachers we have worked with have found them to be more than sufficient for their needs. The following three build on these and greatly expand the scope of Catch1Partner.

Activity 4: Treasure hunting for answers (and introducing peer learning)

At a glance: In this version of Catch1Partner, learners hunt among their peers for answers to their own questions about a given topic, negotiating formulations and writing down responses as they move from partner to partner. It is suitable for late Key Stage 2 and upwards.

Aside from whatever subject content you are dealing with, the two skills at work here are identifying what you do not know and phrasing a question that will yield a useful answer. None of these are simple skills. Being able to assess your knowledge, or lack thereof, with a modicum of realism is a prerequisite for lifelong learning (academic or otherwise) and a key component of metacognition (which is the topic of Activity 6). By inserting a written element into Catch1Partner, you are securing written evidence of learning within the activity itself, further cementing Cooperative Learning as a teaching tool, not a game.

This version of Catch1Partner follows some form of input, whether a week-long project on the Second World War, a 30-minute YouTube video on the Aztecs or a flip-chart presentation on persuasive texts by the teacher (see Figure 2.7).

Figure 2.7. Learners note down their questions as the teacher presents input.

Make available appropriately sized pieces of paper and something the learners can use as clipboards (a hardcover book will do) or use erasable mini-whiteboards. Then ask them to write down their name and list all the things on their paper that aren't clear to them about the input – for example, '**I'm not sure** if Japan was an Axis power,' '**I don't know** when the Aztecs lived' or '**I can't remember** what "thesis" means.' To most learners, this is not as simple as it seems. If necessary, scaffold the task with helpful starter phrases (examples in bold above) and elicit examples from the class. (Indeed, it a good idea when you do this for the first couple of times to restrict them to yes/no questions or questions with single answers.) Recognising what you don't understand or are uncertain about is a high point of metacognition. Some learners will simply draw blanks and will need lots of support to identify even one thing from the oceanic gaps in their knowledge, resulting in the comprehensive and utterly unhelpful 'I don't know anything.'

A way around this is to provide an inventory of questions (cleverly aligned with your intended outcomes) which learners can copy to prop up their own list as necessary ('Mike, just pick any question you can't answer from the whiteboard and transfer it to your list'). As always, anything is better than nothing. By asking even a teacher-generated question, Mike sees that it is actually within his reach to pose a question, and that an answer not only exists but is also forthcoming. Seek and you shall find.

In the ensuing Catch1Partner, learners attach their piece of paper along with their written questions to their clipboards, grab a pen and hunt for answers among their peers, writing down their statements and their names. Again, you will find ample opportunities to train ancillary skills, such as recognising key points and using concise and precise language in a very life-like scenario. Until a child masters this, he will likely be stuck with the same partner for the full duration of this type of activity.

Here is a rare exception to the rule that we never meddle with the steps in the CLIP. Rather than swapping materials in step 6, learners keep their lists with them at all times. The reason for this is simple: the lists are highly personalised and will not be relevant to anyone else.

Steps 2–3: Partner A poses a question from his/her list and partner B answers. If B cannot answer the first question, A asks another question from the list.

Step 4: Partner A praises and writes down the answer along with partner B's name. B confirms the entry.

Step 5: Partners switch roles, so now partner B asks and partner A answers, B writes down the answer and A confirms the entry.

The pair skip directly to step 7 (Partners bid farewell and proceed from step 1), setting off to find new partners.

Figure 2.8. Treasure hunting for answers: steps 2–7 of Catch1Partner with their various tasks.

For the sake of individual accountability, make sure that the learners write their partner's name next to any answer they give (see Figure 2.9). In some classes, it may even be advisable to have the learners literally sign their names next to the written version of their answers. This inculcates a sense of responsibility in both partners: for the questioner to check his understanding and faithfully write down the response verbatim, and for the respondent to formally assume bold responsibility for his answer.

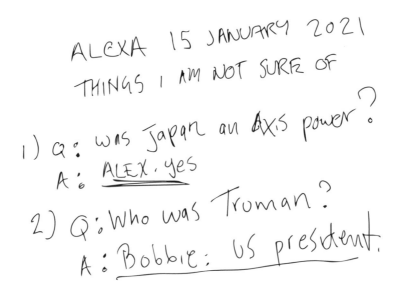

Figure 2.9. A sample learner's list of questions with responses from named peers.

Why are we doing this, Miss?

The main objective(s) of this exercise is to secure individualised evidence of knowledge gaps and close as many of these gaps as possible through peer-to-peer learning. (In this way, you don't have to do it all over again; remember that you've just spent time and effort presenting the knowledge to them – let them demonstrate their learning.) Secondary objectives related to you as a teacher include gaining an insight into how complex misunderstandings occur, all the better to tackle them, and not wasting time correcting sloppy misunderstandings (e.g. 'If the Romans were so clever, why didn't they just use machine guns, Steve?' 'Bobby, the Romans did not have machine guns because machine guns were not invented until modern times – like when they made steam trains and stuff!').

Ancillary objectives for learners also include identifying knowledge gaps, formulating relevant questions, asking and answering to the best of their ability, taking responsibility for explaining their answers as required by each partner, assessing and challenging the quality of partners' responses, and faithfully writing down acceptable responses.

Furthermore, this activity will demonstrate to learners how Cooperative Learning promotes interdependence and helpfulness among peers. It may be useful at this juncture to discuss with your learners the deep interdependence in workplaces, families and human societies in general to build their character (or whatever it is called in the current guidelines).

Materials

A4 paper, clipboards (or similar transportable hard surface), possibly a bulldog clip to hold the paper in place, pens or pencils and erasers, or simply use erasable mini-whiteboards. (There is no printing, no photocopying and no laminating for the teacher – what's not to like?)

Consider in advance what to do with their written products. We have given some ideas for their use in a plenary following the 'After the activity' section. But ask yourself: are these lists of questions and answers glued into their books? Are they handed in? Are the written products copied onto a large classroom poster for everyone's benefit? Forget the CLIP; ask yourself what you would normally do. Regardless, take the opportunity to look them over, address any misconceptions and use any particularly good questions and/or answers as examples to be emulated.

Staging your activity

There is a lot going on in this activity. The more complex the activity, the more having rigorously drilled the basics of Catch1Partner will pay off in spades. We have reminded ourselves about Rule 1 (Scaffold the subject task) above. As for Rule 2 (Be specific about what you want them to do), make sure the following points come across to your learners:

+ Only ask for one answer from each partner. The reason for this is that otherwise all the higher-attaining pairs will stay glued together during the entire activity, going through their numerous clever points, leaving lower-attaining learners without the benefit of their input.

+ If your partner cannot answer the first question on your list, simply ask the next question until you find one he can answer.

+ If your partner is unable to answer even a single question, never chide him or her. On the contrary, thank and praise him for giving you the time to ask.

+ There is no problem in asking the same question to multiple partners, especially if you are a little bit unsure about the validity of the first response you get. Comparing answers provides useful fuel for discussions. For example, which sounds most reasonable: Kung's claim that the First World War started in 2014 or Agneta's claim that it was, in fact, 1914?

+ Feel free to ask clarifying questions about a response you get.

+ There is no problem in presenting an answer you have acquired from a previous partner if you are asked a relevant question, as long as you mention from whom. In our class, we give everyone their due!

For Rule 3 (Show, don't tell) especially, make sure you overdo the demonstration when it comes to not swapping materials, as learners will assume this is a given if you have been doing lots of revision with flashcards or open questions where swapping is crucial. It goes without saying that you are scrupulously monitoring the question-writing process, as this gives you lots of opportunities to assess their understanding, prompt deeper thinking, promote quality questions and so on. One benefit of keeping track of the writing process is that you can focus your in-activity monitoring on the learners with questions that yield the greatest insights into the learning process.

Instruction-checking questions

Below are some examples of how to turn your instructions into questions (and confirmations):

+ 'How many answers should you get from each partner?' ('That's right, one!')
+ 'What will you do if your partner cannot answer the first question on your list?' ('That's right, simply ask the next question until you find one he can answer.')
+ 'Will you chide your partner for being unable to answer?' ('No, on the contrary, thank and praise him for giving you the time to ask.')
+ 'May you ask the same question to multiple partners?' ('Yes, it's fine, especially if you are a little bit unsure about the validity of your first response.')
+ 'May you ask clarifying questions?' ('Yes!')
+ 'Is it OK to give an answer you have acquired from a previous partner?' ('Yes, as long as you give credit where credit is due.')

And furthermore:

+ 'Should we write down our partners' answers?' ('Yes.')
+ 'What do we need to bring from our desks?' ('Lists, clipboard, working pen/pencil/ eraser.' As usual, before the activity starts, say: 'Hold your materials above your heads, everyone – let's see them! Lists! Clipboard! Pens!')

Plus any others you think are relevant for the specific class and subject area.

During the activity

Monitor, monitor, monitor. Know what you are looking for in relation to clear assessment criteria and take full advantage of the written element by looking over their shoulders rather than simply listening in. As always, demand that your instructions and directions are rigorously followed: if you tell the learners to write down the name of the individual who gave them the answer, they do need to write down the name of the individual who gave them the answer. Whether learners are aware of it or not, this allows you to track critical misconceptions back to their source and further boosts individual accountability, as noted above.

Note: If you have a class where people try to land each other in hot water by writing nonsense answers and attributing them to their peers, let pairs confirm by hand-signing their names on each other's notes.

After the activity

By gathering learners' lists of questions and answers, you will have ample raw material for a highly focused plenary. We advise that you give yourself time to go over the answers, possibly while the class is busy with individual work. Look for themes: which questions were the most common? Which questions were answered? Which questions were mostly left unanswered? Was there an especially interesting question? Do any of the questions indicate serious gaps in their learning or your teaching?

By combining information from the learners' Q&A notes with what you overheard as you were monitoring, you are in an ideal position to devise a short plenary on what is actually important: 'Most of you asked about …', 'Many of you erroneously believe that …', 'I am very pleased to see that you were able to answer …'

Again, make sure that the evidence is retained by gluing it into their books, photocopying it or whatever you normally do. If you do want to go there, this activity demonstrates the progress learners are making in each lesson: 'At the beginning of the lesson, Kurt wasn't sure when the First World War started. At the end of the lesson he was informed that it started in 1914, and now has that written down. This information was passed to him by Agneta.'

Note: Keep in mind that this activity is not primarily about providing you with summative assessment (which could be done in a million other ways). It is about teaching your learners a wide range of skills that they will need in other contexts, the two main ones being to identify gaps in their knowledge and to formulate questions to unpick these knowledge gaps.

When do I take the next step?

When you are able to stage and run the activity effectively, including the variation that learners no longer swap materials but instead write down answers from named peers (with a signature if you deem that necessary).

Activity 5: Integrating learners' products in Catch1Partner

At a glance: Learners produce personalised and relevant Catch1Partner materials under teacher supervision which are fused with the wider learning process. During production, Catch1Partner may provide peer-to-peer quality control.

Every teacher has anecdotes about how their learners lose costly materials, spill food on them or drop them on the floor and step on them. Usually, the result of such vandalism is that the good-hearted TA spends her time photocopying a new set for little Johnny. Alas – no more, little Johnny!

In the Cooperative Learning classroom, learners are gradually made co-responsible for their learning. This entails reaching a point where the learners can generate materials aligned with the teacher's objectives that are personalised, relevant and add yet another opportunity for teacher/peer/self-assessment. As you will recall, individual accountability is at the core of Cooperative Learning – the 'I' in PIES. This procedure promotes responsibility, not only for their own learning process but also that of their peers. Therefore, any and all materials produced by the learners are signed and dated, not only because 'we take pride in our work', but because any errors will be tracked back to their source. It is useful to think of this as a teaching and learning process, rather than something we need to get done so we can move on to the actual activity.

Figure 2.10. Front side of a card by a Year 4 pupil (anonymised). Note the erased shadow of a former iteration of the card.

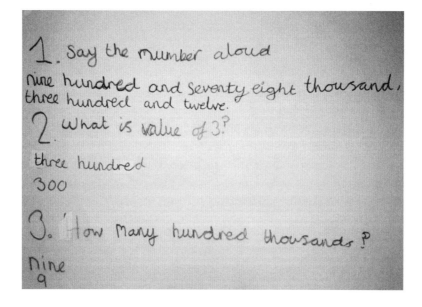

Figure 2.11. The back of the same card: the three tasks added over time along with their answers. Again, note the corrections. Creating teaching resources is a complex process for a learner.

When integrating learners' products in Cooperative Learning activities, the connection to direct instruction is a matter of life and death. The sample card by the Year 4 pupil (Figures 2.10 and 2.11) represents the application of a great deal of learning, and hence a great deal of teaching. The first and most obvious reason is that an unguided production process potentially embeds and exponentially spreads unchallenged misconceptions in what should be permanent resources. This is a big step up from simply writing a list of questions and getting feedback, which we saw in the previous activity. However, the peer feedback element they mastered above can be utilised effectively here (yes, transferable skills!). Therefore, our usual step-by-step example – starting with 'Why are we doing this, Miss?' – presents Catch1Partner as a peer assessment tool where the peers critique each other constructively. The second reason we promote the connection between activities and direct instruction as a matter of life and death is that it forms the bedrock of an unparalleled holistic teaching and learning experience. This is best demonstrated through a practical example: see Ms Schmitt's German MFL class at the end of this activity.

Whenever possible and relevant, learners' materials should be laminated and reused indefinitely across the whole school. A school community does not merely exist in the physical space designated by the school itself and the buildings in the catchment area. It also exists in time. Not only do most UK schools cater to a chain of siblings, many of them also cater to generations. In these days where the intangible World Wide Web has left many children (and adults for that matter) adrift and disconnected from a life with other people, knowing that thousands of learners over many years, including your little brothers or sisters, and possibly your sons or daughters, will benefit from your work, helps learners to understand they are part of a bigger picture.

Why are we doing this, Miss?

As important as it is to provide children with a meaningful life narrative, it is usually a secondary objective in a school setting because you are teaching a curriculum limited to specific subject matter, such as maths, English or science. Fortunately, Cooperative Learning can facilitate both objectives simultaneously.

If you have followed the roadmap above to embed Catch1Partner, you are more than ready to start using it to facilitate your own objectives using materials produced by your own learners. Always remember that Cooperative Learning serves to accomplish the outcomes you desire and is not a reason to reinvent any wheels.

When learners begin to produce their own materials for Catch1Partner, stick to simple rapid recall or basic procedural tasks, so you can take as a model the Q&A cards you made for them in the second activity. Pick content that will never be removed from the curriculum, such as identifying word classes, number bonds and so on. Explain to the learners that the days of teachers and TAs doing their work for them are numbered, as well as the importance of what they are doing and the benefit their work will bestow on future generations: 'Your children and children's children will see your work.'

Cooperative Learning is nothing without your decisions, so grab a pen and write out on a piece of paper your objective and envision what you want their ideal product to look like. (Hint: pick a key area where you know the learners need to improve their rapid recall.)

My main objective(s): _____

My ancillary objective(s): _____

Here is an example from a primary maths teacher:

My main objective(s): Learners memorise number bonds to 10. Each child will have produced one signed and dated flashcard with an intelligible question written on one side and the correct answer on the other side.

My ancillary objective(s): Learners should include the number bonds as dots to be counted.

Then draw several examples of what you want ideal cards to look like, and reflect on the ideal answers you would like your learners to give, the extension tasks, the opportunity to embed vocabulary or review prior knowledge – anything and everything that connects to the core task. Kill a million birds with one stone.

Figure 2.12. The front and back of a card drilling number bonds to 10. Note the punctuation mark to distinguish this card from number 6. Note also Simon's signature and the teacher's counter-signature and date. This card may be used in several ways. 'What is the number bond to 10?' works for both sides. You can also ask learners to hold up the card, covering the 1, and ask their partner to count out the bond, rather than using the dots as mere support for struggling learners.

Here is an example from a secondary history teacher:

My main objective(s): Learners memorise key facts/names/dates in the chapter 'The Age of Industrialisation' on pp. 33–42. Each student will have produced one signed and dated flashcard with one fact extracted from that chapter on one side and an appropriate question to elicit said fact written on the other side.

My ancillary objective(s): Learners should connect, contrast or compare their selected fact about the age of industrialisation to life today.

Main objective example: A model of a flashcard.

Question on front: What are the 'red brick' universities?

Answer on back: Between 1900 and 1909, red brick universities were founded in Birmingham, Liverpool, Leeds, Manchester, Sheffield and Bristol. They concentrated on 'hands-on' courses, such as science and engineering, as opposed to traditional university subjects like history.

Ancillary objective example: An ideal illustration of connecting, contrasting or comparing (to be modelled to learners before the activity).

Red brick universities were an early version of what we now call vocational train-ing. If red bricks were set up today, I think they would be teaching you to become an electrician or a gas engineer.

Aside from clarifying your objectives, this process provides you with worked examples and prepares you for modelling the ideal behaviour and interaction to the class.

Materials

When using learners' products as materials in Catch1Partner, something a bit more sturdy than plain paper may be called for. Consider light-coloured cardboard which can cope with a lot of erasing and greasy fingers. Consider whether your objectives are best served by you cutting out the cards in advance or making learners do that too (bearing in mind that pre-cutting allows you to get straight to the production of subject content).

Make sure the cards are a good size and appropriate for all the content you plan should be on there eventually. Remember that Cooperative Learning is not a one-size-fits-all ven-ture: if a specific learner's handwriting requires a bigger card, give him a bigger card. And make sure the learners draft their cards using pencils, not pens. You need to allow multiple stages of correction before anything is committed to ink and, potentially, teacher signature and lamination.

As you are responsible for the teaching, it is your responsibility to scaffold the production of the materials in a way that minimises risk, so you need to give ample opportunity for assessment and corrections to each card by multiple partners before the final, signed prod-ucts land on your desk.

The simplest way to approach peer correction is to drop their first flashcard draft into the previous 'treasure hunting' activity. However, in this case, the task is not to answer your partner's list of questions relating to certain teacher input, but rather to assess and suggest improvements to your partners' newly produced flashcard. In a nutshell, use Catch1Partner as a peer assessment tool, where the peers give each other constructive criticism.

Note: As a quick alternative to fancy learner-produced flashcards, simply ask them to use as input some independent work they have to hand (including home-work) and ask them to compare, discover differences and discuss their answers during the Catch1Partner. As in Activity 4, they obviously do not swap materials, as the main objective is for them to assess the quality of their own work. Zero prep-time in class and an approach that has demonstrated its effectiveness.[22]

Staging your activity

In this activity, securing uniform, high-quality materials is all-important, so the production of cards should be seen as an element of scaffolding the subject task (Rule 1). Draw up an ideal card on the whiteboard using small steps and show where the information on the card has come from. If your lesson resembles the secondary history lesson from page 73, discuss how to turn a statement into a question and answer. Specifically, discuss the importance of limiting the scope of the question and guiding the respondent towards the answer (see Steve and Ludmilla's conversation on page 79). Demonstrate the significance of legibility, font size and wording. Recap any and all special characters or vocabulary they need to use. This is also important for learners to communicate effectively when offering suggestions during peer learning to identify and clear out basic errors. If you are asking them to make flashcards that will teach shapes, for example, recap terms such as *angle*, *edge*, *parallel* and *acute*. Make sure all the necessary information is clearly visible on a whiteboard, poster or flip chart at all times. There must never be any excuse for learners to back out and say, 'I don't know'. Knowing your class, you may decide to further differentiate support for specific learners, such as grouping them with a TA, picking out specific/simpler content for weaker individuals and so on.

To further minimise misconceptions going into the first production draft, make sure they have access to all relevant support materials, whatever the subject might be: books, dictionaries, previous notes, multiplication tables, lists of dates, definitions of word classes, indexes of shapes, rulers or compasses. Remember, this is not a test: the objective is to quickly and effectively produce high-quality classroom resources. The fact that the cards double as assessment tools is secondary.

---

22 In his original article on the most effective teaching strategies, Rosenshine specifically mentions 'having students correct each others' papers, and asking about points on which the students had difficulty or made errors': Rosenshine, Principles of Instruction, 13.

Think in advance about task distribution. If you are asking a Year 2 class to produce a card set for the 2 times table, the chances are high you will wind up with 30 cards with '1 x 2 = ?' on the front and '2' on the back. A simple way of getting around this is to write either a question or an answer on the card in advance and let the child with that card work out what goes on the other side. For example, for a lower-attaining pupil you might give the question '2 x 4 = ?' and let him dig out his multiplication table, write '2 x 4 = 8' on the back and sign his name. For a gifted and talented pupil, you might simply write '8' and leave him to work out the question and add the '2 x 4 =' to your '8' before signing his. You can also ask specific groups of learners to sample their card data from specific chapters, pages or paragraphs to ensure a broad scope ('Maya's table, you extract facts only from chapter 1, Ji-hoon's table only from chapter 2, Ali's table only from …').

As for the format of the flashcard, there are two approaches: one option is to repeat the question with the answer – for example, question: 2 x 4 = ? and answer: 2 x 4 = 8 (see Figure 2.13). This visually connects the question and the answer and helps any distracted children remember what the question was.

Front   Back

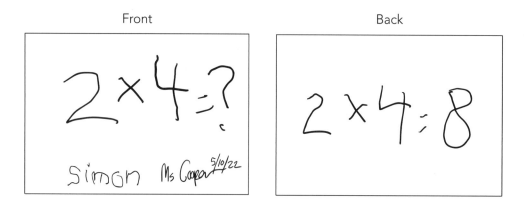

Figure 2.13. Repeating the question on the back can help learners to make connections between the question and the answer.

The other option (see Figure 2.14 on page 77) gives you more flexibility: noting down only the answer on the back of the card allows you to vary the difficulty of the activity by picking which side of the card is the question – for example, rather than asking: 'What is 2 x 4?' the learner now has the option to show the other side and ask: 'What can you multiply by 2 (or 4) to make 8?'

Front   Back

Figure 2.14. Not repeating the question on the back offers more flexibility.

Always make sure that you give them sufficient time to create their flashcards as individual work, as opposed to a group endeavour, to ensure you know where the misconceptions are coming from and to inculcate individual accountability. 'But this was Sandra's idea!' simply will not do.[23]

Do not embark on Rule 2 (Be specific about what you want them to do) before the first iteration of the cards is ready for assessment, or they will forget what you have told them because their minds are occupied with production. Small steps always. At this juncture you have a choice. One option is to weed out basic problems as you circulate and monitor their work – 'basic problems' meaning cards containing unintelligible nonsense, lacking an answer on the back and so on – and then launch the activity. However, in theory, as long as they have an answer and a question, you could set them off unchecked to get feedback from their peers. In this case, pre-correcting everything before you run the peer learning activity means you may actually miss out on differentiated learning opportunities. As always with Cooperative Learning, it is about taking a step back to step in more efficiently. Do what is best in your situation.

If the learners are peer checking the materials, make sure when you model the task that you demonstrate relevant questions that partners could ask each other based on your

---

23 If/when you get around to using Word-Rounds (described in Appendix A), ask the learners to take turns presenting and critiquing their cards within their home team before sharing them with the wider class. This adds an extra 'sloppy mistake filter' and prepares them for discussions across the class.

knowledge of the class and your monitoring of card production. Here are some suggestions:

+ Is the language appropriate?
+ Is the writing legible?
+ Is that word spelled correctly?
+ Is the question clear?
+ Is the answer clear?
+ What could be the difficulties for your peers with this card?

You could also suggest some relevant non-threatening starter phrases:

+ May I suggest that you ...
+ I see what you mean, but ...
+ I may be getting this wrong, but ...

Remember, these are only suggestions: you understand your class and your situation better than anyone.

Presenting your work is always a vulnerable moment (Rule 3: Show, don't tell). It's important that praise, especially when suggesting improvements, is clearly modelled. It may be helpful to make use of the Education Endowment Foundation's support triangle here, which scaffolds learners' interactions with TAs from correcting and modelling through to prompting and self-scaffolding: in the same way that you don't want TAs to spoon-feed learners, you also want to get rid of the bibs in peer-to-peer learning.[24] Finally, remember that this is an instance where the learners do not swap cards because they are hunting for as much feedback as possible to reflect on and enhance their own products.

Example of a teacher modelling peer-to-peer critique of card production in Catch1Partner

Steve is a history teacher in Key Stage 3. He has modelled both sides of an ideal card on the board:

> Question: What British raw material provided power for the Industrial Age?
> Answer: Coal.

---

24 See Sharples et al., *Making Best Use of Teaching Assistants*, p. 15.

He has also created another card which he will use to demonstrate good feedback to a common error:

Question: What happened before the 1800s?

Answer: Education was not free and poor children got what education they could in dame schools or Sunday schools.

Modelling a sample feedback dialogue in front of the class, Steve puts the question up on the whiteboard and calls up Ludmilla, a student, to model the feedback dialogue:

Steve: Hi Ludmilla, I've made this draft card. Can you give me some feedback, please?

Ludmilla: Sure, let's hear it!

Steve: OK, so the question I have put on the front is: 'What happened before the 1800s?'

Ludmilla: Uh, what? Well, like in the Stone Age or …?

Steve: No, come on, Ludmilla, you know this assignment is on the Industrial Age!

Ludmilla: OK, hmmm … Let me think. OK, before the 1800s Britain wasn't such a big empire yet!

Steve: No, look! The answer is: 'Education was not free and poor children got what education they could in dame schools or Sunday schools' *[he turns the card over and brings up the statement on the whiteboard behind them for the class to see]*.

Ludmilla: But how am I supposed to know this is about education from your question? It could be about anything. I mean, everything that happened before the 1800s happened before the 1800s, right?

Steve: So, you think my card doesn't work?

Ludmilla: Well, yes and no. I see what you mean, and I think it's a good and relevant piece of information about education in the Industrial Age, but I also think you need to work on the question. Remember what the teacher said about 'limiting the scope' and 'asking guiding questions'? Look at that first example on the board about coal. Can you see how the question, 'What British raw material provided power for the Industrial Age?' points to the type of answer? You see, the answer can only be a type of fuel.

Steve: Right, so instead it could be like: 'What education could poor children get before the 1800s?' What do you think of that?

Ludmilla: Let me see the answer again … 'Education was not free and poor children got what education they could in dame schools or Sunday schools.' Yeah, that actually works quite nicely, you know. Brilliantly done, Steve!

Steve: Thanks, Ludmilla. I couldn't have done it without you. May I see your card now?

Ludmilla: Yeah, sure, so the question on my card is: 'How did the slave plantations help the Industrial Revolution?'

Steve: Well …

In his final commentary before posing his instruction-checking questions, Steve reiterates the importance of limiting the scope and, of course, lauds Ludmilla for using one of the non-threatening phrases from the permanent 'polite conversation' poster Steve has stuck on the wall, 'I see what you mean, but …' to soften what could perhaps be perceived as purely negative feedback.

Instruction-checking questions

You are now more than capable of choosing your own instruction-checking questions. For example, think back on the rationale of allowing only one comment from each learner: 'How many answers should you get from each partner?' ('That's right, one!'). Similarly, address any specific issues that make this activity difficult or are crucial to effective execution.

During the activity

You know the drill: monitor, monitor, monitor. In general, only intervene to deal with off-task behaviour. Any and all interventions should be short and to the point. Stay on the lookout for general themes that you will need to unpick in future.

After the activity

There are several things that can be done when the learners are finished with this Catch1Partner: their work can be assessed by a number of peers, ideas for improvement can be logged (with the name of the partner who helped) or the teacher can move on to the next areas of learning. However, there may be two groups – those who did and those who did not pick up cues from their peers.

Learners who received no critical comments now present their peer-checked work to you and, pending your endorsement, they immortalise it using a permanent pen. Otherwise, it's back to the drawing board. (Make a note to yourself that not one peer picked up on this misconception – does this need to be addressed?) Finally, put your own signature on the finished card next to theirs. With this final stamp of approval, the card is ready to be included in the Hall of Eternal Fame, also known as 'the plastic box where our flashcards go' – after the holy ritual of lamination, should you so desire. If this can be done without breaching safeguarding regulations, get the learners to do this too.

While this is happening, learners who did get suggestions for improvement from peers spend their time working these into their cards – and when they feel ready, they can go through the above vetting process with you. At the end of it all, you should have at least one homemade signed and sealed flashcard for each learner in the class, all organised around a specific theme, whether that is simplifying fractions, historical dates or scientific terms.

> **Note:** There is no reason why flashcards cannot include drawings, diagrams, shapes, photos and so on – whatever achieves your objectives. Just balance out the time it will consume to produce the cards with how much the learners will benefit, how much you can assess from this work and how often these materials will be reviewed.

When do I take the next step?

When your learners consistently demonstrate that they are able to produce signed and dated flashcards to a high standard (i.e. they are not only legible but also within the scope you have defined and phrased so as to make sense to the potential reader) and, of course, you and they are able to run the activity effectively. No avoiding specific peers, no pushing/spitting/shouting/kicking/cussing, no hiding in corners, no off-task conversations. Have high expectations of yourself and your learners. If teachers and children in the worst schools in the worst areas of austerity-blighted Britain can manage a reasonable level of manners and engagement, so can yours. You and your learners deserve to feel safe, appreciated and in control in the environment where you spend so many of your waking hours.

Once the flashcards are ready, they may be used in Catch1Partner for basic rapid recall, laced with context-generating questions or anything else that will drive the learning to where you want it to go. Please refer back to the previous activities.

Integrating teaching, learner-produced materials and Cooperative Learning

We mentioned earlier in this chapter that connecting direct instruction with Cooperative Learning is a matter of life and death when using learner-produced materials. Aside from blocking misconceptions that spread during production (dealt with above), intelligently interlacing the two gives you and your learners a unique opportunity for a highly effective and holistic teaching and learning experience, where very small components are reviewed in detail, embedded as 'muscle memory' and finally stitched together over time into comprehensive schemata.[25] Through Catch1Partner, skills are drilled, knowledge is presented, checked and counter-checked, and gaps are identified and closed with every learner by every learner, simultaneously. When your direct instruction is in order and your learners know how to run the steps, a CLIP like Catch1Partner outguns and outmanoeuvres any other approach to guided practice in terms of efficiency.

It is worth noting here that these activities do not dispense with the need for individual practice; in fact, the aim of any Cooperative Learning activity should be that each and every individual, regardless of levels or labels, is able to demonstrate their new learning on their own. You will find more on the theories underpinning the relationship between guided and individual practice in Chapter 3, but the following section gives an example of how teaching, material production and Catch1Partner may go hand in hand.

Jakob's heart is in foreign language teaching and he has often made use of learner-produced materials in Catch1Partner, especially at Key Stage 3 where learners have (hopefully) built up more resilience and a sense of communal responsibility. The following is an example of staged deployment of learner-produced materials for Catch1Partner, transplanted to a Year 8 German class.

---

25 When we talk about 'muscle memory' we are, of course, referring to Ofsted's draft *School Inspection Handbook*: 'Pupils also need to develop fluency and unconsciously apply their knowledge as skills' (p. 44).

Ms Schmitt's German MFL class: a multi-lesson vocabulary and grammar review

In her German MFL class, Ms Schmitt has identified 30 common verbs which continue to cause trouble for her learners. She plans some dedicated revision and reviewing: in small stand-alone units over multiple lessons, her learners are to go through several cycles of production and use of materials within Catch1Partner, with varied tasks, in order to commit these verbs, along with their pronouns and application, to long-term memory.

Verb mastery requires rapid recall of their meaning, the pronunciation of all their conjugations and the virtual muscle memory of their application. This is a tall order, so to start off Ms Schmitt has made each of her learners responsible for just one single verb, including its pronunciation, which they are required to drill at home using selected online resources. This distribution supports individual accountability and a sense in each learner of adding unique and essential value to the class as a whole. Knowing her class and her subject, Ms Schmitt assigns the more complex verbs, such as the modals, to her top-tier students.

Mindful of cognitive overload, Ms Schmitt wisely chooses to limit focus to the present, past and future in the indicative only. Her aim is to build a foundation from which she can safely and easily move on to the two conjunctive forms in the German language. Further to this limitation, the card production itself and the ensuing activities are subdivided into three phases – A, B and C, which are described below. The duration of each phase is dependent on the level and progress of the learners.

The first objective (A) is for every learner in the class to recall, within one second, the meaning and any iteration of at least 80% of these 30 verbs and their pronouns.[26] This does not happen magically by the students running around chatting randomly with inconsistently designed cards. Therefore, as we saw in 'Staging your activity' above, Ms Schmitt presents the subject matter in small, manageable steps. The card design is meticulously modelled on the board (embedded in schemata and with necessary reminders of grammatical rules and concepts) and, using printed sheets with the verbs' conjugations, each learner works individually on transferring their own designated verb in the present tense with pronouns onto a sheet of A4 cardboard, exactly as demonstrated by Ms Schmitt (see Figure 2.15).

---

26 Ms Schmitt's target of an 80% success rate is not arbitrary. It reflects the evidence-based advice found in Rosenshine's 'Principles of Instruction', which her school leader wants to see implemented across the school. Ms Schmitt understands that Cooperative Learning is not a bolt-on, but should always integrate and operationalise other good teaching practices. For more on this see Chapter 3.

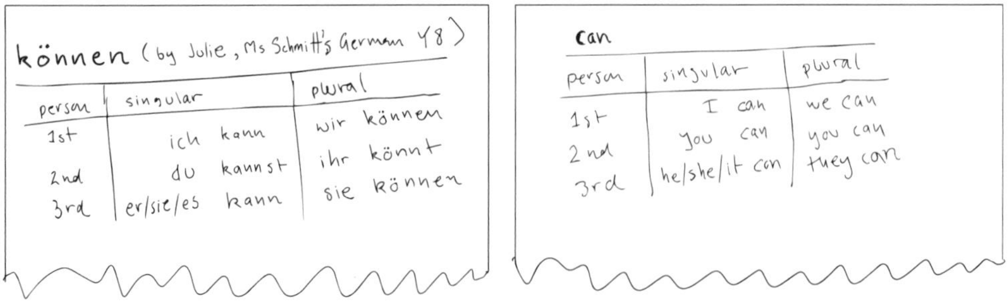

Figure 2.15. An example of the first iteration (to achieve objective A) of a card featuring the German verb *können*. Note the name and class on the front of the card: *können* is the verb assigned to Julie.

As her students work on their cards, Ms Schmitt walks around the class, systematically checking and correcting card content and each learner's pronunciation of the particular verb for which they were made responsible. If we use Julie's card as an example, Ms Schmitt spots that she has forgotten to include the capitalised formal *Sie* on her card, which she has specifically requested all students to do. (Whether or not you chose to run the peer vetting process described above, remember that you cannot allow any misapprehensions to slip into these materials, hence the signature and countersignature once the card has been approved for circulation.)

Below we have described each of the individual phases, which show how direct instruction, learner production and Catch1Partner combine to achieve Ms Schmitt's goals.

Part A: Objective: Rapid recall with correct pronunciation of pronoun and verb conjugation in the present tense

In a number of German lessons, time is set aside for five- to eight-minute Catch1Partners, where the first iteration of the card is used with various tasks, each repeated as many times as needed. Sample tasks and sample answers for each Catch1Partner are listed below in order of deployment:

1. 'What is the infinitive of the verb *können* in English?' (Answer: 'Can.')

    In this first exercise the card-makers keep their cards for the subtask: 'Repeat the pronunciation after me … [models German pronunciation of infinitive form].' (Answer: Mimics pronunciation.)

2. 'What is the infinitive of the verb "can" in German?' (Answer: '*können*.')

3. 'Please conjugate *können* in the present with the correct pronouns.' (Answer: '*Ich kann, du kannst, er/sie/es kann* [and so on].')

    a. Optional subtask: Spot similarities and differences in patterns between our two cards.

    b. Optional subtask: Identify the pattern and list verbs from memory which follow a similar pattern.[27]

4. 'I am going to say a German pronoun. You will instantly add the matching present conjugation of *können*. For example, I say *du* and you say *kann*! Are you ready …?' (Sample question from Julie's card: *ihr* …? Answer: '*könnt*.')

5. (Needs detailed modelling) 'Please make a sample sentence with the present tense of *können* and translate it into English.' (Sample answer: '*Ich kann Deutsch sprechen* [I can speak German].') Note that, as required, cards might include sample sentences with their translations to further limit the chances of spreading misconceptions.

Bear in mind that when they are embedded in a Catch1Partner, the above tasks are simultaneously executed by 30 learners rotating 30 cards with different verbs. With most encounters lasting anywhere from 30 to 90 seconds, even in a five-minute Catch1Partner, each learner is processing four to ten verbs on average. In accordance with good practice, Ms Schmitt runs the same task in as many Catch1Partners as needed, spread over several lessons to achieve spaced retrieval practice.[28] She also uses all observations during the activities to target individual issues on a one-to-one basis, preferably on the spot, and general issues in plenaries, where she also draws out examples of high-quality conversations she has overheard and lauds supportive behaviour. In short, everything we have learned in the preceding activities.

---

27 Previously, Ms Schmitt has taught the patterns of the three types of regular verbs in German (ending in -en, -el/-er and -ten). With this subtask, she is now making sure that her students consciously link back and apply this prior learning.

28 See Carpenter et al., *How to Use Spaced Retrieval Practice to Boost Learning*.

Part B: As above, adding past tense

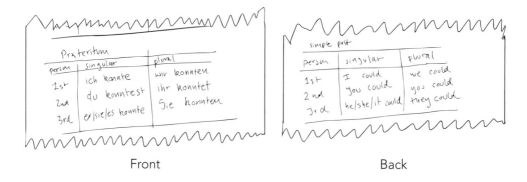

Front   Back

Figure 2.16: The past tense is added under the present tense on the same card.

The simple past tense (or *Präteritum*) is added to the card (Figure 2.16) following the same procedure of direct modelling. In the following couple of German lessons, time is set aside for a number of five- to eight-minute Catch1Partners with various tasks. These include new iterations:

1. 'What is the past tense of *Du kannst*? (Answer: '*Du konntest*.')

    a. Subtask: 'Is this verb regular or irregular? How do you know?'

2. 'Please make a sample sentence with the past tense of *können* and translate it into English.' (Sample answer: '*Ich konnte die Musik hören* [I could hear the music].') Note that, where required, cards might include sample sentences with their translations to further limit the chances of spreading misconceptions.

While the last task in particular would need to be modelled by Ms Schmitt, tasks that are virtually identical (e.g. task 1 for past and present tense) may need no detailed modelling, so she makes an individual assessment of what staging is needed for each new activity to succeed. Just remember that each new task you insert in a Catch1Partner can be viewed as an entirely new activity and therefore may need a new round of modelling: Rule 2 (Be specific about what you want them to do) and Rule 3 (Show, don't tell).

Part C: As above, adding application

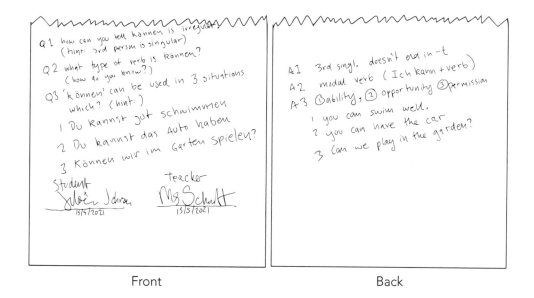

Figure 2.17. In part C, the students finalise the card
by delving into the application of their verb.

Each learner now takes time to investigate their verb in more depth (e.g. Is it a modal? Is it irregular? Is it transitive? What can we say about its application? Ideas to help memorisation?). This is a good opportunity to do the peer feedback exercise that opened this chapter. This gives students the chance to check their ideas and get new ones to put on their card. It is important to present examples on the cards, so the learners can confirm their understanding on the spot. (See Julie's card for sample questions for the verb *können* – Figure 2.17.) Again, if you know your learners and your subject, you will know who should be made responsible for the more challenging items; Julie got a modal verb. It goes without saying that this process requires a lot of teacher modelling and support.

Throughout all the above phases, Ms Schmitt monitors two things: the production of the cards and the execution of the CLIP, especially listening for pronunciation issues. Any individual learner's challenges are targeted then and there, as needed, and general problems are picked up in appropriate full-class direct instruction. Remember, Catch1Partner only constitutes a small part of the lesson. There is ample time for the usual work of reading, writing and speaking, but every opportunity is taken to draw connections to the cards. For example, Charlie is reading the opening stanza of his latest German love poem aloud to the class:

Charlie: Du sagen meinen namen.

Ms Schmitt: Stop right there, Charlie. What's the regular verb conjugation of second person singular *du*?

Charlie: Oh sorry, Fräulein Schmitt. Right, it's *+st*, so my sentence should be, 'Du *sagst* meinen namen.'

Ms Schmitt: Who is responsible for *sagen*? Nidal, that's you! Is Charlie right?

Charlie: Ja, Fräulein Schmitt.

Ms Schmitt: Good! Charlie, continue …

And beyond

With the indicative present and past firmly embedded, learners now have the basic knowledge needed to master the formulas for the more complex tenses in the indicative and two conjunctives. The *Partizip* forms are added to the cards and Ms Schmitt goes through one formula per lesson. For example, she presents the formula for German *Futur I* ([present tense of *werden*] + [infinitive of the main verb]) with lots of worked examples and she warns about common errors, such as never directly translating the English phrase, 'I am going to [verb]'. As each item is presented, it is immediately drilled in Catch1Partners, during which learners apply their new knowledge to their completed verb cards (which have all the information needed to form any tense once you know the formula). Ms Schmitt demonstrates the interaction with a student, modelling questions, hints, answers and thought processes, while recapping the basic skill she is trying to teach. All Ms Schmitt's worked examples are clearly visible during the activity, along with sentence stems for peer support and all the other elements of good practice discussed in previous chapters. Here are some sample tasks for a selection of tenses:

1. 'Tell me how to form a *Futur I* tense of [infinitive German verb – in Julie's case, *können*] in the indicative and give me an example.' (Answer: 'To form the *Futur I*, you insert *werden* in the present before the infinitive form of *können* – for example, "*Ich werde können …*" [I will be able to …].')

2. 'Tell me how to form a *Futur II* tense of [infinitive German verb] in the second conjunctive and give me an example.' (Answer: 'To form the *Futur II* in the second conjunctive ...')

3. 'Tell me how to form a *perfekt* tense of [infinitive German verb] and give me an example.' (Answer: 'To form the *perfekt* ...')

Obviously, Ms Schmitt adds subtasks to hammer home any concepts she finds her students struggling with – for example, after task 2:

> 'Remind me when to use the second conjunctive, please.' (Answer: 'Mostly for indirect speech or to express imaginary situations, dreams, suggestions and recommendations – for example ...')

Again, we cannot sufficiently express the importance of the teacher's direct instruction and modelling.

Real German MFL teachers might find that this level of detail seems well beyond most secondary students' capacity and, indeed, the common expectations of GSCE levels. However, our point with these examples is that if you interlace Cooperative Learning with direct instruction – especially the building of schemata, so all of the elements being reviewed are connected in a well-organised mental framework (e.g. the *Futur I* vs. *Futur II*-type subtask) – then the drilling, negotiation and application in the activities at each successive stage will give the learners mastery of a stunning amount of knowledge and skill sets.

The above is but one example. Ms Schmitt could equally apply the card production process directly to complex grammatical structures. In this scenario, each student is made responsible for a tense (e.g. *Futur II* or *Plusquamperfektum*) rather than a specific verb. Counting all tenses in the indicative and the two conjunctives, Ms Schmitt needs about 14 cards. The complexity of this task when compared to simply copying conjugation sheets means that students benefit from working in pairs or groups. Here a Think-Pair-Share would be a neat way to provide quality control.

Our point is that these examples are simply a handful of ideas in the ocean of possibilities. You know how best to connect learners' card production to your direct instruction, if/when to add more content and which tasks and subtasks to use to add value to their cards over time, the frequency of the activities and, crucially, how you slot all these elements together over time to create progression.

Activity 6: Metacognition through Catch1Partner

At a glance: Use Catch1Partner to discuss and investigate the process of learning to train metacognition and self-regulation.

Metacognition and self-regulation is the second-highest ranked strand in the Education Endowment Foundation Toolkit, weighing in at an average of seven months of additional progress per learner per year.[29] For the record, we want to point out that Stalham Academy has not dedicated their Catch1Partners to metacognition specifically. However, in one of the most successful Strategic School Improvement funded projects in the (all too brief) history of that programme, Jakob specifically designed Cooperative Learning training to drive metacognition through CLIPs.[30] We present this section to give you the option and to exemplify how Cooperative Learning may act as a delivery mechanism for a wide scope of less concrete approaches. Again, you will need to apply your own good judgement to your situation.

What is metacognition? According to the Education Endowment Foundation, 'Metacognition and self-regulation approaches aim to help pupils think about their own learning more explicitly, often by teaching them specific strategies for planning, monitoring and evaluating their learning.'[31] Note that metacognition obviously does not take place in a vacuum, so this activity is launched at relevant points in a learning process. Like Activity 3, this activity uses open questions. Materials consist of cards with generic metacognitive questions. There is no answer on the back as the objective here is to promote learners' awareness of their own learning processes and inculcate specific metacognitive strategies, modelled by the teacher before the activity.

---

29 See Education Endowment Foundation, Metacognition and Self-Regulated Learning; and A. Quigley, D. Muijs and E. Stringer, *Metacognition and Self-Regulated Learning: Guidance Report* (London: Education Endowment Foundation, 2018). Available at: https://educationendowmentfoundation.org.uk/public/files/Publications/Metacognition/EEF_Metacognition_and_self-regulated_learning.pdf.

30 J. Werdelin, 'Don't Worry, Dad … Now I Can Teach You Maths!' – the Success of the Gender Gap SSIF, *cooperativelearning.works* (11 June 2019). Available at: https://cooperativelearning.works/2019/06/11/dont-worry-dad-now-i-can-teach-you-maths-the-success-of-the-gender-gap-ssif.

31 Education Endowment Foundation, Metacognition and Self-Regulated Learning, p. 1.

It is important to note that you can embed metacognition as a part of any Catch1Partner: Simply adding the question "How did you work that out?" or "How do you know that?" as a subtask instantly trains metacognition in the context of each specific question the learners come across.

Aside from the obvious benefit of being able to assess learners' understanding of subject content simply by monitoring the discussions prompted by the cards, this activity also facilitates an ancillary objective: to pinpoint who finds metacognition difficult in order to tailor interventions to meet each learner's specific needs. This activity could finish off as many lessons as is deemed useful by teachers and leaders.

Why are we doing this, Miss?

To introduce the concept of metacognition to the learners and, optionally, to get them further involved in feedback. The metacognitive strategies can even be focused on the activity itself to help identify what went well, what didn't go so well and what could be done to improve it.

Metacognitive materials

Materials consist of cards with generic metacognitive questions. If you are looking to run your activity at the end of the lesson in connection with summative assessment, your question cards might be classics like: 'What didn't go well?', 'What could you do differently next time?', 'What went well?' and 'What other types of problem can you use this strategy for?'[32] or more conversational: 'What in today's lesson didn't you get – maybe I can help you?' or 'Did someone help you today? How?'

If, on the other hand, your activity follows direct instructions on a specific task, and is intended to support the following stages of guided and independent practice, your questions might be more along the lines of: 'Does anything in this presentation conflict with your prior understanding? Please elaborate', 'How does this presentation relate to what you have already learned?' and 'What questions will you be asking yourself next time you are working out this type of problem?' (More examples can be found in Appendix B.) Of course, you can find others on the internet or make your own to match an area within your subject or even specific types of tasks.

....

32 Adapted from https://cambridge-community.org.uk/professional-development/gswmeta/index.html.

As the questions and answers are not personally relevant, as normal the learners should swap cards once they have asked and answered each other's questions.

Staging your activity

While most learners can cope when asked about their favourite movie, book or colour, the question: 'What is the most important thing you've learned today?' is likely to send many, even in Key Stage 4, into shock. The response requires a range of reflections, from the definition of 'important', deciding if the question refers to any lesson or to school in general or to personal encounters specifically, and even to remembering what happened five minutes ago, let alone an hour. After 20 seconds of intense thinking, you are likely to get one of two answers: a defiant 'Nothing' or a sheepish 'I don't know.'

This is where your scaffolding comes in – just like when teaching any concept in science, maths or English. A good idea is to present some of these questions in a plenary in advance or make them otherwise visibly available during the lesson so the learners can ponder their mysteries. When you model with a TA (or a carefully selected and prepared learner), try to pick questions that share most similar traits with the set and/or that you think will prove most difficult for learners to answer. In particular, model – and make visible in huge letters – phrases that partner A can use to prompt (in bold below).

A: My question is: 'What in today's lesson did you find most difficult – maybe I can help you?'

B: I don't know.

A: Can you remember what this lesson was about?

B: No.

A: **Well, I remember** that we were learning about fractions. Miss Hamilton asked me a question and I wasn't sure about it.

B: Yes. Um. Fractions.

A: So, **think** about fractions – what do you find difficult?

B: Everything … I don't know.

A: OK, tell me one thing you do know about fractions – it doesn't matter if you aren't sure.

B: The number under the line is the numerator … or the other one.

A: Let's see if we can find help in the classroom. Look at the learning wall.

B: The number under the line is the denominator, I think.

A: So, **now we know** you find the terms for the numbers in fractions confusing. So, what have we learned from this conversation?

B: That I can get help on the learning wall?

A: Brill! What's on your card, then?

B: 'What was the most exiti … ex …'

A: Would you like some help reading the card?

B: Yeah … no wait, I got it, 'exciting thing you … le … lear … learned today?'

A: Well …

Instruction-checking questions

You can add the following to the other relevant instruction-checking questions from previous activities:

* 'What can we say if our partner cannot answer the question?' ('Yes, we can prompt him.')
* 'Where can you find prompts to support your partner?' ('Yes, you can use the phrases on the whiteboard/learning wall/flip chart.')

During the activity

As always, monitor, monitor, monitor. With content that gives such rich opportunities to discover learners' perceptions of their own learning, consider organising your observations into a rota to focus on two or three learners in every lesson to ensure that your attention is equally distributed. Where applicable, TAs must be involved here too.

After the activity

Metacognition provides unique opportunities to discuss learning beyond individual subjects. It also allows you to build up that elusive character trait resilience, not because learners are told to stiffen their upper lip and carry on, but because they are equipped with tools that allow them to traverse obstacles by consciously drawing on previous experiences and strategies. However, this trait is not taught as a discrete lesson (Metacognition?

Check! Moving on!), but learned through constant use, day after day after day, directly in connection with specific subject content.

The questions sets we have provided in Appendix B are generic and best used after the teacher has presented new knowledge or a new procedure. However, other cards sets focus on reading, writing, listening and speaking, collaboration, roles in learning environments and so on. Simply google 'metacognitive questions' and see what pops up. Print, cut and there you go!

It may be beneficial to follow up each activity with an open plenary, discussing and assessing learners' experiences during the activity, such as finding answering particular questions difficult. Learners should be a part of identifying and implementing best practice – it is their classroom, after all.

The six activities presented above should let you stage and run Catch1Partners with various materials to achieve a wide swathe of objectives. The following two chapters on direct instruction and social construction look at these individual activities in the larger context of teaching and learning.

Chapter 3

Cooperative Learning and Direct Instruction

The most successful teachers spent more time in guided practice, more time asking questions, more time checking for understanding, [and] more time correcting errors.

Barak Rosenshine, 'Principles of Instruction'[1]

When we do training in schools, people are often initially surprised at the amount of emphasis we place on the teacher's role: 'Wait, isn't Cooperative Learning supposed to be student centred?'

For a range of reasons, the late American professor Barak Rosenshine's short 2012 paper, 'Principles of Instruction', has reached international fame and his text is a useful tool to contextualise Cooperative Learning in the larger scheme of a lesson. Just as there is an unhelpfully simplistic understanding that Cooperative Learning means *student-centred* learning, there is an equally simplistic equation made between Rosenshine's principles and *teacher-centred* learning in the form of direct instruction.

In the first case, Cooperative Learning supposedly implies that students should drive their own learning by unleashing their enquiring minds, formerly held back by outmoded teaching styles. In the latter, Rosenshine supposedly espouses the idea that the teacher should stand by the board and fulfil the role as the sole fount of knowledge in the classroom. However, as we shall see in Chapter 4, it is more nuanced (and more helpful) to see direct instruction as the teacher sharing her 'expanded inner voice' as a model for the learners to develop their own inner voices in the following phases of guided and independent practice.

1   Rosenshine, Principles of Instruction, 16.

In fact, Cooperative Learning intimately either connects to, or directly facilitates, a very great number of Rosenshine's principles. For example, teachers should 'ask students to explain what they have learned'. They should also 'provide many examples' and a 'high level of active practice' and they should 'check the responses of all students' to 'provide systematic feedback' and intercept misconceptions throughout the lesson.[2] Unfortunately, with an average classroom teacher–student ratio of 1:30, running meaningful teacher–student dialogue is impractical, so in reality only a small handful of students get detailed responses and contribute in a class forum. This is the antithesis of Rosenshine's recommendations. Here, a well-chosen Cooperative Learning Interaction Pattern (CLIP) may help to achieve some of Rosenshine's key principles.

Instruction powers construction

Looking at the other side of the coin, well-chosen direct instruction enables the CLIP to run effectively. After all, what stops teachers benefiting from 30-odd peers learning from each other? It is the usual suspects of paralysing 'What are we supposed to do's?', off-topic conversations, off-task behaviour and omnipresent domination and evasion common to unstructured group work, where the stress of management far outweighs the sketchy chances of useful learning outcomes. This is precisely why schools should adopt Cooperative Learning: to reap the benefits of peer learning without these drawbacks. As we have seen, CLIPs require no teacher planning to enforce individual accountability, positive interdependence, equal participation and simultaneous interaction, making Cooperative Learning the opposite of chaotic group work.

However, effective organisation of peer interaction is not in itself sufficient to achieve the desired learning objective; the fact that learners participate equally does not mean that their contributions are useful or even that they are able to contribute at all. On the contrary, in many cases the learners, especially in low-attaining areas, simply have no impulse to speak or act and so either act up or shut down in response to the seemingly hopeless task of presenting their thoughts on this or that topic. (Indeed, Jakob has worked in schools where asking students to describe their morning routine was deemed by teachers well above Key Stage 3/4 cognitive and communicative capacity.) This is why we need to return to Rosenshine's principles: any task performed in a CLIP needs 'models of

---

2   Rosenshine, Principles of Instruction, 19.

worked-out problems' and 'with clear and detailed instructions and explanations' – and many of them.[3]

The point is that Cooperative Learning does *not* equate with doctrines around social construction which, in their most extreme iterations, seem to require learners to reinvent wheels that have been a thousand years in the making. On the contrary, when Cooperative Learning follows proper direct instruction, learners present and negotiate their understanding of a narrow subject area based on the teacher's modelled examples ('This is how to … identify a verb/thread a sewing machine/convert a fraction/form a question in French/apply Ockham's razor … now you try!') and are provided with relevant scaffolding. In terms of thinking processes, not least those pertaining to metacognition and self-regulation, learners benefit from the verbalisation of the teacher's own thought processes as the task is presented.[4] This goes beyond generic 'oracy', as such scaffolding might include subject vocabulary, sentence starters or even whole phrases, modelled in context by the teacher. You have seen all of this in practice in the preceding activities. In terms of materials, scaffolding might include access to reference books, worked examples on the board or learning wall, dictionaries, Numicons, calculators, internet searches and so on.

Application to all subjects is possible because CLIPs are void of content. As you will recall, CLIPs only organise children's interaction by controlling who acts or speaks at a given time and place. It is the discussion or the task the CLIPs facilitate that makes them subject or age specific. But within that, individual CLIPs may be more or less versatile. Some CLIPs are designed to promote one very specific outcome (e.g. procedural task resolution, reading comprehension, presentation), whereas others focus on soft skills (e.g. active listening, interviewing, presenting, giving feedback, debating, conflict resolution). Finally, a CLIP such as Catch1Partner is more of a jack of all trades. For this reason, a teacher with a repertoire of CLIPs needs to select them and their content, duration and position in the lesson stream carefully to match her intended outcomes.

The upshot is that Cooperative Learning is not a lazy teacher approach. Aside from being required to teach from the board (and to set relevant tasks pitched at the right level within the specific CLIP and to time the activity appropriately to levels and intended outcomes), teachers are specifically required to monitor closely as their learners start talking. Children and young adults will be a lot more candid about their misconceptions with one peer than with the teacher in front of the whole class.

---

3   Rosenshine, Principles of Instruction, 19.
4   Sherrington, *Rosenshine's Principles in Action*, p. 20.

That said, once the simple step-by-step routines that constitute the CLIPs are mastered by teachers and learners, Cooperative Learning frees up cognitive capacity for the actual art of teaching – especially processing the rife opportunities for formative assessment to give live feedback and identify next steps. It also frees up cognitive space for the art of learning. The steps in each CLIP are the same every day (and always yield the benefits described above), leaving learners free to focus exclusively on the actual subject task. (And yes, we are indicating here that Cooperative Learning helps to reduce cognitive load; Catch1Partner automatically slices learning into a series of manageable bite-sized blocks.)

Turning Rosenshine's principles into practice

Incidentally, a recent work on Rosenshine is Tom Sherrington's *Rosenshine's Principles in Action*, where you will find a reference to a classic CLIP – the aforementioned Think-Pair-Share – in his chapter on questioning. If you want to 'ask more questions to more students in more depth'[5] (or, indeed, operationalise the majority of his other principles with much work on the part of your learners and without too much on yours) what you want is well-executed Cooperative Learning.

Jakob often promotes Sherrington's book (and the associated poster designed by Oliver Caviglioli[6]) to the schools he works with because it compresses Rosenshine's principles into four manageable chunks: (1) reviewing, (2) questioning, (3) sequencing concepts and modelling, and (4) stages of practice. The following is a quick outline of how Cooperative Learning supports each of these elements.

Reviewing

+ Daily review.
+ Weekly and monthly review.

Catch1Partner's most obvious strength is in effective reviewing and its reduction of cognitive load (as we saw in Activity 2). The ease with which you can review large volumes of material in the five to eight minutes advised by Rosenshine is in itself sufficient reason to use Catch1Partner every day. It has been a staple at Stalham Academy since it was

---

5   Sherrington, *Rosenshine's Principles in Action*, p. 39.
6   See https://www.olicav.com/s/Rosenshine-Principles-red-anke.pdf.

introduced in the first twilight session, and the impact on retention and application is mind-boggling.

Rosenshine specifically mentions 'having students correct each others' papers, and asking about points on which the students had difficulties or made errors'.[7] This is the essence of Activity 5, where not only might you use custom-made lists of challenging items but also drop in any type of completed task, from sample sentences to maths worksheets for comparison and discussion. Thirty children, all at once. In a five-minute activity, in a 30-strong class, each learner would have 75 minutes of engaged discussion (i.e. five minutes x 30 learners (divided by 2 for pairs)); all high quality because it is based on the preceding modelling of your thought processes.

Questioning

+ Ask questions.
+ Check for student understanding.

Catch1Partner is about asking questions, and many of them. As a bare minimum, each card lets the learner pose one question to their partner. You can have as many questions as you have learners, or you can choose to replicate the same few questions on multiple cards. You can also choose any type or range of questions you want, spanning from the generic metacognitive to the closed and narrowly subject specific. You can even add on subtasks, such as: 'When you have answered your partner's question, say what you would have done in this situation and why', to add punch to a set of revision flashcards about the actions of fictitious or historical figures.

In this dialogue about the Tudors, Benny reads out from his card: 'What did Henry do when he discovered Anne Boleyn had been unfaithful?'

Andrea: He had her executed.

Benny: That's correct. And what would you have done?

Andrea: Hmmm, I think I'd have executed her too, because otherwise my people wouldn't like, you know, respect me as a king … like, *The Crown*, yeah? But it's still wrong though … but, hey, it must actually be difficult being a king. You have to make all those decisions … Now it's my turn to ask you a question.

....

7   Rosenshine, Principles of Instruction, 13.

Benny: OK.

Andrea: Why did Cromwell ...?

Added to this, of course, is your opportunity to throw in a question to an individual during the activity which provides differentiation without slowing down the rest of the class. ('Good thinking, Callum. But what stops the Queen today from executing Prince Andrew, who also undermines people's respect for the Crown?' or 'What quote about just that do you remember from *Richard III?*') If you want a high volume of opportunities to ask questions, get answers and discuss and assess understanding, Catch1Partner should figure prominently in your toolbox.

> Teachers also can study their students' thought processes by asking them to think aloud during problem solving.
>
> **Barak Rosenshine, 'Principles of Instruction'[8]**

Sequencing concepts and modelling

+ Present new materials using small steps.
+ Provide models.
+ Provide scaffolds for difficult tasks.

These concepts are the very foundation of successful Cooperative Learning, and also happen to be the direct instruction to which Rosenshine's principles are sometimes reduced. These elements are detailed in Chapter 2, especially in the subsection 'Basic rules of staging an activity', and then again in relation to each sample activity.

Stages of practice

+ Guide student practice.
+ Obtain high success rate.
+ Independent practice.

---

8   Rosenshine, Principles of Instruction, 18.

The cognitive processing of the preceding direct instruction that takes place within Catch1Partner – in the case of revision, well scaffolded by the answers on the back of the cards and supported, checked and augmented by the negotiation and visible worked examples left on the whiteboard with peers – *is* guided practice. You are not on your own yet. Running through a five-minute Catch1Partner where you apply a skill gets you ready to sit down by yourself with a worksheet (independent practice) and crunch tasks. Note that Sherrington advises 'corrective and affirming feedback' during guided practice.[9] However, unless you have another adult present for the overarching monitoring (or your learners have reached a level where you trust they will stay on task while you delve deeply into a conversation with specific pairs), stick to single-sentence, ultra-brief interventions during activities, as we have advised previously. However, you, and only you, know how to balance comprehensive formative assessment against individual support in your specific activity on a given Thursday afternoon.

There is yet another reason why monitoring is a priority. One important element of good teaching is to drop learners from guided practice into individual work at the right time: not too soon (or they will struggle individually and you will stress around trying to plug gaps) or too late (wasted time, boredom and high risk of off-task behaviour). Walk around, look and listen. Some teachers find it helpful to have a signal to indicate that pairs are successful, such as high-fiving if they both get the task right. By monitoring the very public guided practice in Catch1Partner or other CLIPs, you will know when it is time to move on to individual practice.

And there you have it. Each of Rosenshine's principles, as summarised by Tom Sherrington, neatly interlaced with Cooperative Learning. Not a bolt-on, not a gimmick; rather, a complete model of what is required to get the maximum impact from your direct instruction.

---

9   Sherrington, *Rosenshine's Principles in Action*, p. 62.

Chapter 4

Cooperative Learning and Social Construction

What a child can do with assistance today, she will be able to do by herself tomorrow.

Lev Vygotsky, *Mind in Society: The Development of Higher Psychological Processes*[1]

It should be reasonably clear from the preceding chapters that Cooperative Learning refers to a specific classroom practice and therefore does not equate with social construction any more than it equates with the vague concept of student-centred learning. Certainly, in the context of this book, social construction is not a classroom practice but rather a theory about how humans learn at certain phases in the lesson, most notably the guided practice stage of the process. So, there is a connection between Cooperative Learning and social construction, and understanding this connection will further enlighten why direct instruction is so crucial to successful Cooperative Learning. It will also give some background to Drew's ingenious Teaching and Learning Cycle, which has been so foundational to the success of improving schools. In this chapter, we offer a quick peek into the mechanics of the learning operating behind the sleek show of the Cooperative Learning activities themselves.

---

1   L. Vygotsky, *Mind in Society: The Development of Higher Psychological Processes* (Cambridge, MA: Harvard University Press, 1978), p. 87.

The history of the inner voice

Social construction as an educational theory is usually attributed to the Russian psychologist Lev Vygotsky. In the 1930s, Vygotsky put forward the notion that from earliest childhood our minds are shaped by social activity (i.e. interacting with other humans) and that what he termed our 'inner voice' develops in the 'zone of proximal development'. This zone is the learning space just beyond our reach, and expanding it requires a 'more knowledgeable other' to demonstrate things, including modelling the use of language. Over time, Vygotsky conjectured, the adult voice depletes and learners go off on their own to develop their own inner voice, which in essence is consciousness itself. Happily, this process also happens to be the very essence of learning itself, and hinting at the aforementioned importance of direct instruction, the single indispensable and more knowledgeable other in the classroom happens to be you, the teacher.

> Another form of scaffolding is thinking aloud by the teacher.
>
> Barak Rosenshine, 'Principles of Instruction'[2]

Types of inner voice

In the 1970s, the development of the concept of the inner voice was further investigated by Russell Hurlburt using a technique which entailed sampling the thoughts of people whenever a beeper went off. His experiments offered more insight into the various forms of inner voices. These forms are perhaps best documented by researcher Charles Fernyhough, who defines three categories of inner voice: the expanded, the dialogic and the condensed.[3]

The *expanded* inner voice is basically the same as external speech with all that comprises an individual's grammatical idiosyncrasies. An example from the classroom is procedural work, which after first being learned can be attested and practised. A more personally relevant example of the expanded inner voice is the sort of internal monologue you might

---

2   Rosenshine, Principles of Instruction, 18.
3   C. Fernyhough, *The Voices Within: The History and Science of How We Talk to Ourselves* (New York: Basic Books, 2016).

have had when your driving instructor was teaching you to change lanes at high speed: 'OK, I need to change lanes – that truck up front is way too slow … Need to start now … Don't panic, check mirrors … Is that blue car behind me going to overtake the truck as well? … I need to wait, maybe … Should I wait? … No, he is turning off at the junction … Aaaaah, too close to the truck, break! Break! Phew! Check mirrors again, indicate, always keep eyes ahead, don't stare at the truck as you pass …' You will recognise the terms 'check mirrors', 'don't panic' and 'always keep eyes ahead' as the internalised voice from the more knowledgeable other – in this case, your driving instructor.

Alongside and linked to the expanded inner voice is the *dialogic* inner voice. During functional MRI-type brain scans, participants were asked to imagine a conversation between themselves and someone else – which in itself is an important element in developing thought. The scans revealed that imaginary inner dialogues, as far as the brain is concerned, are similar to real communication with another person. Being aware of this and imagining a conversation with someone else can help a learner to assess the value of an idea – for example, why the Romans managed to dominate the antique world or the validity of applying a specific mathematical procedure to a word problem. In essence, the dialogue, whether internal or external, acts as a mirror in which (self-)reflection takes place. Back to when you were a novice driver: 'Hang on, when I want to change lanes on the motorway, am I meant to check the side mirror before or after I start indicating? Well, it stands to reason you need to check the mirror before, because if you start indicating with someone speeding along next to you, he might get nervous and swerve.' The imagined answer represents the synthesised teaching of the driving instructor, now fully internalised and merged with the self-confidence of experience.

Again, the cooperative learning classroom offers endless opportunities for learners to experience real dialogue which can provide the building blocks for the development of their own dialogic inner voice. Indeed, access to such modelling in the home (such as simple conversations about the news or the day's events over dinner) is a key factor in academic success. The language and vocabulary gap between wealthier and poorer children is already apparent at 18 months of age, and by the age of 5, children from the most disadvantaged backgrounds are 19 months behind their better-off peers.[4] Also, variations in tasks and partners afforded by Cooperative Learning activities mean that peers will sometimes find themselves in the role of the learner and sometimes in the role of the more knowledgeable other. For a lower-attaining pupil especially, the latter experience is exhilarating.

---

4   National Literacy Trust, *Language Unlocks Reading: Supporting Early Language and Reading for Every Child* (2019), p. 8. Available at: https://cdn.literacytrust.org.uk/media/documents/Language_unlocks_reading.pdf.

This leads us to the final category, *condensed* inner speech. This is an abridged and non-grammar-based composite which is unique to each individual and makes up how we recall a process, see an answer to a process or just remember something. For example: when multiplying by 10 or 100 or 1,000, Drew just thinks 'zeroadd' in his brain. Drew would never explain it in that way to a class, but for the majority of practical day-to-day aspects that is how his condensed inner voice often operates. It is built and dependent on the knowledge of expanded speech; in some ways, certainly in the educational environment, it is the outcome of compressing previously expanded speech. Interestingly, and further research beyond this anecdotal example supports this, sometimes Drew can just see the zero appear at the end of a number and then the thought is devoid of a voice, thus attesting to Fernyhough's contention that the condensed voice doesn't always replicate speech in the perceived sense.

Ultimately, the transition to ever more condensed inner speech speeds up the thinking process. A pertinent example of this from your own experience might be the fact that you can now change lanes at 70mph while singing along to the radio and planning which objectives you want to achieve with your next iteration of Catch1Partner. Your inner voice, which helped you to work through each painful step of changing lanes under the watchful eye of your driving instructor, is now so condensed that it operates as subconscious muscle memory. If this is not an 'alteration in long-term memory', what is? The process just needs practice, which is where Cooperative Learning really shines.

> Progress ... means knowing more (including knowing how to do more) and remembering more. When new knowledge and existing knowledge connect in pupils' minds, this gives rise to understanding. As pupils develop unconscious competence and fluency, this will allow them to develop skills, i.e. the capacity to perform complex operations, drawing on what is known.
>
> **Ofsted, *School Inspection Update: January 2019, Special Edition*[5]**

The research on the inner voice is not finished (doubtless it never will be), but in educational terms the influence of this work is clear. Combining Cooperative Learning with an awareness of inner speech – the teacher's role as the more knowledgeable other who is demonstrating the subject content and modelling the thinking process – enables 30-plus

---

5   Ofsted, *School Inspection Update: January 2019, Special Edition* (2019), p. 5. Available at: https://assets. publishing.service.gov.uk/government/uploads/system/uploads/attachment_data/file/772056/School_inspection_update_-_January_2019_Special_Edition_180119.pdf.

learners to simultaneously formulate and refine their own inner voice in presentations and/or dialogues with peers. This is one of the key benefits of breaking a big class into groups or pairs: small units allow a lot more children to practise explaining their thought processes. CLIPs turn up the volume on articulating this inner speech.

As the process of learning (the relatively permanent change in long-term memory) cannot be observed, oral presentations and discussions during CLIPs provide a mechanism that sheds light on the darkness of learning in real time. Thereby, Cooperative Learning provides each learner with instant feedback from peers, based on your direct instruction (and, at a pinch, one to one from yourself) as the more knowledgeable other. Feedback, you will remember, is the highest yielding strand in the Education Endowment Foundation Toolkit. This also serves to explain the relentless focus on 'checking for understanding' in the previous chapter on Rosenshine's principles of instruction.

Summary: The more we become aware of our learners' inner speech and the more we allow its controlled verbalisation in a safe, controlled environment (such as a well-ordered Cooperative Learning classroom), the greater our ability to actively nourish the thought processes of our charges. In so doing, we can have greater control over how and when to move learning on, but, more importantly, how to engage the consciousness of all learners. Small groups allow the time to explore at different levels, unlike the often rushed classroom-level conversations between the teacher and one learner.

To hammer home the vital connection between this chapter on Vygotsky's principles of dialogue and the previous chapter on Rosenshine's principles of instruction: in Rosenshine's scenario, the teacher is the more knowledgeable other who is sequencing concepts and modelling through direct instruction, all carefully designed to be just outside the zone of proximal development, easing the learner towards first guided and then independent stages of practice, as the learner's inner voice becomes more and more fluent and finally takes over from the teacher's.

The Teaching and Learning Cycle

The Teaching and Learning Cycle (Figure 4.1) is a visual model to conceptualise for the teacher the process of learning described above. Based primarily on research into the impact of direct modelling on the construction of knowledge,[6] the Teaching and Learning Cycle works on a macro and micro scale: it can be seen as a model for a scheme of work, an individual lesson or even the stage of a lesson. The context and modelling quarters would apply to the direct instruction phase of sequencing concepts and modelling. CLIPs can be dropped in at any point where joint construction applies, matching the guided practice phase. The joint construction itself can be done in other ways; it does not have to be a CLIP (but then you could use Bing rather than Google).

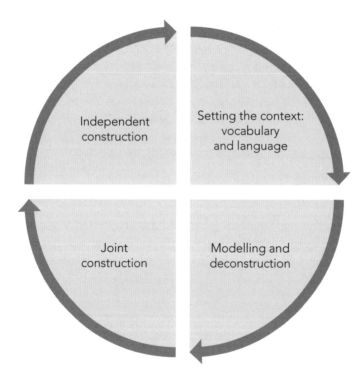

Figure 4.1. The Teaching and Learning Cycle.

6   See M. Halliday, Towards a Language-Based Theory of Learning, *Linguistics and Education*, 5(2) (1993): 93–116; N. Mercer, *The Guided Construction of Knowledge: Talk Amongst Teachers and Learners* (Clevedon: Multilingual Matters, 1995); and P. Gibbons, *Scaffolding Language, Scaffolding Learning: Teaching Second Language Learners in the Mainstream Classroom* (Portsmouth, NH: Heinemann Educational Books, 2002).

An example of joint construction is the following verbatim account recorded in a mixed Year 3/4 maths class doing a Catch1Partner. As we have pointed out already, direct instruction is part and parcel of the Cooperative Learning classroom, and what is clear from this account is how Cooperative Learning supports the vocalisation and training of the pupils' inner voices, based on the teacher's modelling. Bear in mind that this is one of 14 dialogues, and in the span of a five-minute Catch1Partner learners may easily have two or three such encounters, each refining and condensing each person's inner voice towards mastery.

In this activity, pupils had a range of cards with fractions on them (please note that these are two of ten representations of fractions, including other shapes all divided into equal parts). The first task for partners was to identify the fraction using the subject vocabulary (e.g. *whole, part, equal, denominator, numerator*) used in context during the direct instruction and in the exemplary dialogue in the demonstration with a TA of the activity itself. The objective of this activity is not simply to 'get pupils talking'. It must be seen as one among many targeted activities within a sequence of lessons, which builds on the prior learning to help form schemata.

Once the fraction has been identified (e.g. $^2/_6$), the subtask was to see if there was an equivalent fraction to it. Once the learners have mastered the basic steps of Catch1Partner and are confident about the basic task, it is useful to add such subtasks to deepen thought, explain reasoning and make connections. Obviously, any such additional tasks should be modelled and any worked examples left visible during the activity, as noted previously. In this case, the preceding direct instruction of the teacher and the modelling of sentences allowed for the transcribed discussion.

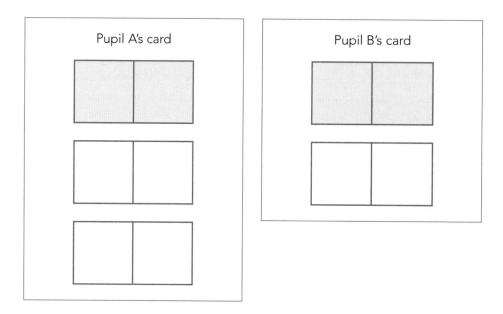

Figure 4.2. Fraction cards showing ²/₆ and ²/₄ respectively.

Pupil A: Hi, can I ask you a question, please?

Pupil B: Yeah.

Pupil A: What fraction have I got?

Pupil B: The whole … you've got … 1, 2, 3, 4, 5, 6 bits that are the same … so that'd be the bottom nominator.

Pupil A: Denominator.

Pupil B: Yeah d'nomnator … and two of the bits are coloured in so that's the numerator, so it's 2 over 6 or two sixfs.

Pupil A: *[Checks board for second question]* Is there an equivalent fraction?

Pupil B: Yeah.

Pupil A: What is it?

Pupil B: Well, there's three blocks that are the same and if you don't look at them lines … then you get one shaded … coloured of it is 1 over 3 or one-third.

Pupil A: Thank you.

Pupil B: What have I got?

Pupil A: You've got 2 over 4 which is two-quarters because I looked at them and there's four equal bits and two are coloured in. But I know that when I look at it I can see that I've got half grey and half white, and I know that half of 4 is 2 because it's like equal bits.

This is a small snippet of dialogue – an example of one of 14 separate but similar conversations going on in the class at the time, scaffolded with phrases supplied by the teacher which influenced and provided one idea about what the learners might say. In terms of altering long-term memory, we can see hints of prior knowledge creeping into context, such as when pupil A uses the link between 'half of 4' which had been taught or learned conceptually in Year 2 and practised using Catch1Partner, among other CLIPs. After the Catch1Partner and some more instruction on conceptual and procedural identification of equivalent fractions, the pupils working individually made some very interesting and, for want of a better word, accurate identification of equivalent fractions within the multiples with which they were comfortable (largely, 2, 3, 4 and 5, with some derived facts and connections being made, such as 18/27 being equivalent to two-thirds).

Can you say for certain that these pupils were fully able to identify all equivalent fractions after that lesson? No. Were they able to find something without the prior instruction of the teacher? Probably getting there, depending on a host of other factors. Is this one Cooperative Learning activity guaranteed to make changes in long-term memory? No, but it certainly helps. What we can say is that this example snippet of dialogue is part of a long journey and the outcomes achieved in the following individual work were certainly influenced by the quality of the direct instruction and the opportunities the CLIP provided for developing and practising a thought process and encouraging links to be made.

This brings to mind a definition of learning by Soderstrom and Bjork that is not too far away from the one found in Ofsted's draft *School Inspection Handbook*, which, when applied to the context of the above example and the need to change long-term memory, chimes well with the purpose and ethos of this book: 'The primary goal of instruction should be to facilitate long-term learning – that is, to create relatively permanent changes in comprehension, understanding, and skills of the types that will support long-term retention and transfer.'[7] 'Relatively permanent' is a fantastic phrase that seems almost oxymoronic but actually encapsulates the idea of learning. People 'learn' something, and unless

---

practised regularly the 'how to' – the recall – becomes a little rusty and is subject to change and reimagining. In essence, Cooperative Learning supports the creation of relatively permanent change and is a vehicle for practice, reflection, making links and consolidating thought.

Chapter 5
The Roles and Responsibilities of Cooperative Learning
What's in It for You and Everyone Else?

Unless you are a school leader, you don't need to read every section in this chapter. Just find the part that relates to your role and understand how this is relevant to you. However, if you are a head teacher, governor or MAT chief executive officer considering Cooperative Learning as a whole-school approach, every section is a must-read because you are the shepherd of your flock.

What's in it for the teacher?

In a short period of time, Cooperative Learning helps to develop seemingly less effective teachers into more effective teachers, and effective teachers into highly effective teachers. Not because Cooperative Learning is brilliant in its own right, but because it simplifies and organises classroom practice to give any teacher a unique opportunity to shine. This entire book is a guide to put teachers firmly in the driver's seat, while shifting the heavy lifting on to the learners.

Precisely because the kids are responsible for the learning, you as a teacher will find your mind space free to be more intuitive, creative and make better decisions in relation to your responsibility for the teaching. You should make use of this opportunity because successful Cooperative Learning requires you to know your outcome, know your learners and know your materials.[1] Engaging with Cooperative Learning is a unique opportunity to rethink and refocus your life as a teacher, if you are so inclined.

In a simple, organised teaching and learning environment, where the same basic activities generate wholly different outcomes across subjects day after day, it is easy to see what is good and less good. There is no clutter to disturb self-assessment. There is a shared language and real practical solutions to real practical problems.

Are they going off-task in your activity? Well, maybe you gave them too much time for a simple task. Are they staring at each other instead of working? Well, you likely set the level too high or didn't scaffold appropriately. Pupil with SEN refusing to engage? Did you remember to give him special rights that would enable him to participate? Problems are easy to spot, and correcting any (or all) of these issues is relatively straightforward. The best thing is that because the comprehensive communication makes the learning process so visible, you can intervene within 30 seconds of discovering something that isn't right. To get the most out of your diminished role as the sage on the stage, you must hone your ability to observe, assess and correct the learning process with the minimum amount of intrusion.

Cooperative Learning puts the learners in charge of the learning, but, more importantly, this is preceded by putting the teacher in charge of the teaching. You need to know your intended outcomes, master your subject, pick your materials and know your learners. To reiterate a key message from previous chapters, Cooperative Learning does not automatically equate with social construction, which assumes that children will arrive at your lesson objectives virtually by themselves through self-organising peer learning.[2] On the contrary, after spending his entire life studying effective teaching and teachers, Rosenshine concluded that the very best teachers provide lots of instructional support by modelling, guiding student practice, helping students when they make errors and providing for sufficient practice and review.[3]

Our point is that there is no conflict between the guide on the side vs. the sage on the stage. The best Cooperative Learning practice requires the teacher to move seamlessly

---

1   Having to choose from a whole catalogue of different CLIPs takes Cooperative Learning to a whole new level. This may confuse the newcomer, who is still struggling to master the basic principles of selecting appropriate content, staging, scaffolding and monitoring the activity. This is the main reason for opting to present only one CLIP in this book; understanding the variations of Catch1Partner is sufficient challenge for the beginner. Once you have more experience, you can successfully transfer your skills to the other CLIPs listed in Appendix A.

2   See J. Werdelin, Deconstructing the Progressive–Traditional Dichotomy; A Note to Mr Peal, *cooperativelearning.works* (26 December 2014). Available at: https://cooperativelearning.works/2014/12/26/deconstructing-the-progressive-traditional-dichotomy-a-note-to-mr-peal.

3   Rosenshine, Principles of Instruction, 12.

between teacher focus and learner focus, and to make sound choices about when to do what. In this context, Cooperative Learning simply ensures that children stay on task and that their learning processes are observable at every step, so the teacher can make informed decisions at every twist and turn of the lesson.

Unlike teaching from the board and sampling a few eager pick-me-Sir's, Cooperative Learning makes gaps in learners' knowledge and their lack of skills instantly and painfully visible, requiring the teacher to take action. This is not a lazy teacher approach. But it is empowering.

What's in it for the early career teacher?

The early career teacher, perhaps, stands to benefit more from Cooperative Learning than any other member of teaching staff. Starting out as a teacher is a vulnerable time and requires support and structure.

As Cooperative Learning provides a shared language and very practical and clear-cut coaching opportunities, it simplifies the feedback from mentors and colleagues. No complex explanations are needed because the steps of the Cooperative Learning Interaction Patterns (CLIPs) look identical across all year groups and subjects.

'In Sage and Scribe yesterday I lost track of who was doing what. Seriously, they were all over the place! What should I do, Mrs Johnson?'

'Well, Maria, get the Sage to stand up, clasp his hands behind his back and look important, and add, "Is the Sage going to sit down?" to the instruction-checking questions. That generally solves the problem.'

To an outsider, this makes little sense; to Cooperative Learning practitioners familiar with Sage and Scribe, this conversation is all you need to completely rewire the activity. (Sage and Scribe can be found in Appendix A.)

Conversely, when leaders deploy Cooperative Learning across your school, you will find that many ECTs latch on to CLIPs for dear life and often become your most heroic champions. In a nutshell, Cooperative Learning helps new teachers struggling to land the ideals promoted at university during their first couple of years, because it provides the fluffy 'best practice theory' of PGCE courses alongside the tight control needed to actually manage classes, drive learning and secure evidence in a live scenario. Indeed, Stalham had lots of ECTs (37% is a sizeable proportion of any staffing structure) when they set out on their journey with Cooperative Learning. Stalham's ECTs are provided with the CLIP toolkit, lesson structures (see the pyramid model in Chapter 6) and an ethos which allows them to flourish. Indeed, 80% of the ECTs at Stalham from September 2014 onwards have stayed at the school and are key classroom and wider school practitioners who also lead training and moderation.

What's in it for the teaching assistant?

A report by the Education Endowment Foundation famously noted that 380,000 TAs are employed across the country at an annual public cost of some £5 billion, but previous research has shown that for children from poorer backgrounds the impact of TAs was too often negative.[4] To drive the point home, TAs are present in most primary classrooms and, furthermore, often handle interventions with vulnerable children – those with SEN or who qualify for the pupil premium – who have a disproportionate impact on results. In small schools, a bad day for a certain child during those fateful hours of SATs may spell doom.

Given that the highest spending primary schools put more than 50% of their often minuscule budget into their TA pot,[5] and the ever increasing focus on measurable results, one would think that everything else would be put on hold until the issue was resolved, especially as Education Endowment Foundation trials have demonstrated that, when they are well-trained and used in structured settings with high-quality support and training, TAs can make a noticeable positive impact on children's learning.[6] For example, rather than deploy TAs in ways that replace the teacher, the guidance report suggests that TAs should be used in the opposite way – to enable teachers to work more with lower-attaining children and those with SEN.[7] Cooperative Learning supports this by removing the need for the 'teacher at the board' as the object of focus. This allows her to move freely, monitoring and focusing on specific learners or teams as the lesson progresses.

---

4   Sharples et al., *Making Best Use of Teaching Assistants*, p. 6.
5   C. Lough, Wide Variation in School Teaching Assistant Spend, *TES* (27 February 2020). Available at: https://www.tes.com/news/wide-variation-school-teaching-assistant-spend.
6   Sharples et al., *Making Best Use of Teaching Assistants*, p. 19.
7   Sharples et al., *Making Best Use of Teaching Assistants*, p. 14.

Because all CLIPs are replicated with different content, day in and day out, the TA knows exactly what ideal practice is supposed to look like.

However, the danger of delving into a single team or pair of children is the loss of the bird's eye view, which could potentially lead to off-task behaviour, losing the sense of pace and not discovering that the rest of the class is struggling or missing learning opportunities. Here, the TA is worth her weight in gold. Because all CLIPs are replicated with different content, day in and day out, the TA knows exactly what ideal practice is supposed to look like. Because she is present when the task is set up (in glorious detail because the teacher has followed the four basic rules of staging an activity), she will also understand any specific subtasks, language or vocabulary that has been modelled. Even if she does not have dedicated planning time, simply agree with the TA at which times she is responsible for whole-class control, so the teacher can dedicate herself where she is most needed. Alternatively, the role of the TA may simply be an additional voice in a group. When seated in a group of four (as described in Appendix A), the power of an extra adult voice remodelling the teacher's instructions, explaining their thought process and providing detailed language is invaluable for learners.[8]

The simplicity and the fact that every single activity is staged and modelled in detail means the TA is all of a sudden on a par with the teacher, with no need for out-of-class prep time. She knows what the process and result of any Cooperative Learning activity should look like and is fully able to observe, challenge and correct the behaviour and (most of) the task resolution thanks to the detailed direct instruction that precedes the CLIP.

As Cooperative Learning allows more children with SEN to be integrated into the classroom, many TAs will find they are pulled from (often less effective) interventions to spend more time in regular lessons, where they are pivotal because, to all intents and purposes, they perform the role of a second teacher during any Cooperative Learning activity, slicing the teacher-to-learner ratio and allowing teachers 'to work more with lower-attaining pupils and those with SEND', as advised by the Education Endowment Foundation.[9] As for interventions, Cooperative Learning is so simple to learn and deploy that many TAs use CLIPs very successfully in small-group interventions. Again, please refer to 'Making Best Use of Teaching Assistants' on cooperativelearning.works.

---

8   You will find a series of dedicated articles explaining how Cooperative Learning helps to make each of the seven recommendations in Sharples et al.'s *Making Best Use of Teaching Assistants* a lived reality in classrooms at: https://cooperativelearning.works/2017/12/14/making-best-use-of-tas-with-cooperative-learning-index-of-articles/#more-8991.

9   Sharples et al., *Making Best Use of Teaching Assistants*, p. 14.

What's in it for leadership?

For leadership, a Cooperative Learning approach is connected to the culture of a school and some of the systems it then manifests. The culture of the school needs to be seen in three key areas: teaching, assessment and curriculum. The basic premise is that, like Borromean rings, they all interlock – the loss of one ring separates the other two. CLIPs can make the rings bind effectively to each other because Cooperative Learning provides clear access and engagement and a well-organised curriculum. It also means that formative assessment (the 'monitor, monitor, monitor' mantra) is built into the success of any CLIP, including Catch1Partner. Perhaps the most powerful element for leaders is the way Cooperative Learning can simplify performance management. Cooperative Learning not only makes learning visible; more importantly to senior leadership teams, it also makes visible the teaching, and it provides hands-on, instant solutions to many, if not most, problems commonly faced by teachers, e.g. learner engagement, pace, etc. Please refer to the dedicated article Making Best Use of … Leadership; Coaching & Cooperative Learning on cooperativelearning.works.[10] Lastly, it gives school leaders a tool to support teaching and ensure that the modelling and scaffolding is as clear and succinct as possible. Reading this book as a leader, you will find these points implicit and explicit across the various chapters.

---

10 See J. Werdelin, Making Best Use of … Leadership; Coaching & Cooperative Learning, cooperativelearning. works (20 September 2017). Available at: https://cooperativelearning.works/2017/09/20/making-best-use-ofleadership-coaching-cooperative-learning.

What's in it for the SENCO?

Like all SENCOs, Drew had to deal with the fundamental problem that the understanding of 'special needs' in education wrongly presupposes that we have foolproof assessment processes which will correctly diagnose and define the needs of every child. As a consequence, the rhetoric of special needs may be humanitarian but the practice is too often about control and vested interests. Aside from making sure that the paperwork is filled out for all the different monied areas and ensuring that any physical needs are met, on a day-to-day level the SENCO's role ceases.

Since Cooperative Learning means that the needs of all children can be met, every day and in every lesson, it fundamentally changes the nature of inclusion within a school setting. This has had a number of consequences for SEND at Stalham Academy. First of all, Cooperative Learning immediately supported Quality First Teaching,[11] a point driven home recently by Jakob at a training session at the University of East Anglia for a number of schools around Stalham. Generally speaking, as long as the school's assessment, curriculum and differentiation systems are in place, then outcomes can be precisely targeted to individual learners through CLIPs, right down to the finest details of acceptable tone of voice, body language, phrases, eye contact and requests for assistance related to disabilities. (As an added bonus, you can tick the fundamental British values box of 'respect' for disability, saving what is often a fire-and-forget PSHE lesson that is better spent on something else.)

As an effect of the above, the number of visiting SEN consultants and experts who so frequently arrived at the school – vaguely explaining to the SENCO that individual children needed 'more structure', 'less listening time', 'more timed focus work' and 'more options to move around the classroom' – dropped to zero overnight as all these recommendations were already pre-met through CLIPs.

---

11 Quality First Teaching originated in the then Department for Children, Schools and Families' guide to personalised learning which summarises its key characteristics as:
- Highly focused lesson design with sharp objectives;
- High demands of pupil involvement and engagement with their learning;
- High levels of interaction for all pupils;
- Appropriate use of teacher questioning, modelling and explaining;
- An emphasis on learning through dialogue, with regular opportunities for pupils to talk both individually and in groups;
- An expectation that pupils will accept responsibility for their own learning and work independently;
- Regular use of encouragement and authentic praise to engage and motivate pupils.
See Department for Children, Schools and Families, *Personalised Learning: A Practical Guide* (Nottingham: DCSF, 2008), p. 12. Available at: https://dera.ioe.ac.uk/8447/7/00844-2008DOM-EN_Redacted.pdf.

Moreover, as engagement in school life improved and the structures of teaching supported those with additional needs, parents became more interested in their children's learning and home–school communication improved. As any SENCO will know, coordination between school and family is crucial for learners with ASD and attention deficit hyperactivity disorder (ADHD).

Where CLIPs have been most embedded as a classroom ethos, the fewer 'high level' social SEN needs are reported by teachers, the more children make progress and the more teachers are able to deliver the needs of all the children.

There are, of course, many other factors to Cooperative Learning when dealing with SEND, but, for example, Cooperative Learning means that the SENCO can focus on the inclusion of those with disabilities within the day-to-day setting. For more on this, see 'What's in it for your learners?' on page 123.

What's in it for the multi-academy trust?

Within a few weeks in March 2018, Jakob interviewed two head teachers, respectively 25 and 15 days into their journey with Cooperative Learning. As he was editing the footage, he noticed that they both repeatedly used the phrases 'shared language' and 'shared framework'.[12] What they were describing was that Cooperative Learning is broad enough to reflect the most maverick teacher's unique materials, style and personality, yet also gives very clear, practical guidelines to more cautious members of staff. Nonetheless, everyone – from the head teacher through to ECT and TAs – are suddenly able to communicate across subjects, intervention types and key stages because the basic form of the CLIP never changes. This creates a consistency across the school that combines to exponentially increase the impact of the programme.

This observation applies equally to the macrocosm of MATs. Probably the most precarious balance in the MAT system is the relationship between the independence of each school and consistency across the trust. Lean too much towards the individual schools and you have a MAT in name only. Lean too much towards the trust and you risk antagonising school leaders and staff who feel disenfranchised and disrespected.

---

12 J. Werdelin, So Far, So Good, *cooperativelearning.works* (8 March 2018). Available at: https://cooperativelearning.works/2018/03/08/so-far-so-good.

The obvious example is procurement. If each school wants to buy its own unique programme, there are no savings on bulk purchases. Conversely, if there is no buy-in from schools, only ongoing policing from the trust will ensure that any common programme is effectively adopted, leading to a vicious cycle of disenfranchisement and further monitoring. Cooperative Learning provides a one-stop solution to this problem.

From the perspective of the trust, the language and basic activities are perhaps more consistent than any other approach to teaching. As a result, any good practice and specific teaching materials produced or found useful can be shared instantly across the entire MAT. From the perspective of the schools, Cooperative Learning moulds itself to their particular ethos and to the needs of each individual learner in each individual class, corresponding to the unique style of each individual teacher. It also allows each school to continue working with existing successful systems and their paraphernalia.

For MATs based on a culture of respect, flexibility and collaboration, Cooperative Learning is an obvious match which can slot straight into current practice to open up a whole new panorama of opportunities. For MATs labouring under what we might call the 'North Korean syndrome' – characterised by huge leadership pay cheques, top-down unilateral decisions and a lack of consultation and transparency – Cooperative Learning will be 'just another initiative' unless there is a significant will to repent at the top of the food chain.

In both cases, the fundamental principles of positive interdependence and individual accountability need to be recognised and actively embedded from top to bottom. In the instance of North Korean-style trusts, the experience will be very much like chemotherapy; extremely unpleasant but well worth it when, next summer, you are hosting a garden party surrounded by relieved and loving friends and family. For everyone else, the menu just turned five star, which is not to be sneered at. For the same reason, for Research School Networks and any MAT big and bold enough to share best practice based on in-house evidence, Cooperative Learning is an obvious way to find common ground for collaboration. This is beyond the scope of this book, but for those curious to know more about using Cooperative Learning to stage and simplify your own research network, Jakob has written a number of articles inspired by talks given by Professor Stuart Kime at our local Research School.[13]

---

13 See, for example, J. Werdelin, A Piece of Cake: Stuart Kime on Baking Your Own Research Network, *cooperativelearning.works* (19 September 2018). Available at: https://cooperativelearning.works/2018/09/19/a-piece-of-cake-stuart-kime-on-baking-your-own-research-network.

To revisit our two head teachers: another common message was that Cooperative Learning in their schools was not an end in itself, but rather the means to achieve all the other things in their development plans. At no point does this happen overnight. No matter the quality of the MAT, success requires both time and effort. It is the essence of slow-burn leadership which can reap great dividends if leaders understand that they have the means to radically improve outcomes and the quality of life for every child under their care if they are patient and consistent. Everything else is a means to that end, Cooperative Learning especially so.

What's in it for parents?

Rather than simply talking at parents during open evenings, Cooperative Learning activities can be used to help families and carers actively engage and contribute in a controlled and safe environment. Stalham Academy has successfully used Cooperative Learning activities to involve parents in a number of open-school evenings. Importantly, these events also serve to give the parents a direct taste of their child's daily learning experience.

In general, the potential for using the organisational principles of Cooperative Learning to engage and involve parents is a relatively unexplored field. In 2019, Jakob worked with Shared Future CIC, a leading UK specialist on the topic, to open up a dialogue with schools and various organisations (including Ofsted's national director Sean Harford[14]) about the use of participatory budgeting as an exhaustive tool to create a comprehensive, realistic learning experience that would logically involve parents, local organisations, businesses and further/higher education providers. In this programme, Cooperative Learning was the practical tool to retain teacher control and keep every learner on task and supported in the non-linear complexities that realistic learning processes (unfortunately) require. However, in spite of a great deal of initial interest in the concept, no school was able to go ahead before COVID-19.[15]

14 J. Werdelin, Participatory Budgeting in Schools #10: Q&A with Sean Harford Pt. 1, *cooperativelearning.works* (29 June 2019). Available at: https://cooperativelearning.works/2019/06/29/participatory-budgeting-in-schools-10-qa-with-sean-harford.

15 The obvious idea of using Cooperative Learning to control the intricacies of project-based learning is one that has been explored elsewhere in Europe – for example, have a look at https://leapsskoler.dk/english. You can read about the programme in the following article, which also discusses connections to the 2019 draft Inspection Framework and the controversy surrounding project-based learning in the UK: J. Werdelin, Participatory Budgeting in Schools? #1; The Stakes and the Stakeholders, *cooperativelearning.works* (20 February 2019). Available at: https://cooperativelearning.works/2019/02/20/participatory-budgeting-in-schools-1-the-stakes-and-the-stakeholders.

This is not because school leaders do not recognise the value – or, frankly, the burning necessity – of a more lifelike learning experience, especially in secondary schools. The reticence is the result of the intense pressure to deliver measurable results with limited resources. But this state of affairs is all the more unfortunate as there is ample evidence that there is little return on parental engagement efforts without a whole-community, strategic approach and unless this effort is embedded in the school's teaching and learning strategy and development plan.[16] But this is the topic of another book.

What's in it for your learners?

Counter-intuitively, what you as a teacher perceive as tight control of every minute of learning is experienced as exhilarating freedom by the learners. Since social skills form such an integral part of the process, Cooperative Learning builds self-confidence, trust and a shared sense of responsibility.

Invisible children

This is further supported by the time element which often specifies which individual child does the talking in a pair or team. This is one of the main reasons why the architects of Sheringham Community Primary School and Nursery's ambitious and highly successful Strategic School Improvement funding project to improve outcomes for girls in maths made Cooperative Learning the linchpin.[17] Too often, the quiet learners whom you might never notice are the ones who benefit from Cooperative Learning.[18]

Lower-attaining children

Thanks to the four basic rules of staging an activity (see Chapter 2), even the weakest child knows what to do and is able to come up with some form of solution, even if it initially takes the shape of emulating ideas from the board or from peers. In the Cooperative Learning classroom, there is nothing wrong in parroting when needed. Recapping what an

16 L. M. Raffaele and H. M. Knoff, Improving Home–School Collaboration with Disadvantaged Families: Organisational Principles, Perspectives, and Approaches, *School Psychology Review*, 28(3) (1999): 448–466.

17 J. Werdelin, 'Mum Wasn't Good at Maths Either, Love …' Girls, Maths & Cooperative Learning in the Norfolk SSIF Bid, *cooperativelearning.works* (n.d.). Available at: https://cooperativelearning.works/mum-wasnt-good-at-maths-either-love-girls-maths-cooperative-learning-in-the-norfolk-ssif-bid.

18 You will find more on the topic of Cooperative Learning and introverts in: J. Werdelin, Inside Out? Collaborating Introverts, *cooperativelearning.works* (5 October 2015). Available at: https://cooperativelearning.works/2015/10/05/inside-out-collaborating-introverts.

adult or another learner has said demonstrates attention and recall, and rephrasing is even better. Saying something is 100% better than days and weeks of not saying anything, even if what you say is wrong – as long as you get instant feedback, which is naturally facilitated by CLIPs. Bringing their misconceptions into the open and negotiating them is the key to closing the attainment gap. The peer-to-peer learning creates an incredible opportunity to differentiate without the rest of the class having to wait.

Higher-attaining children

This begs the question, what does Cooperative Learning offer the higher-attaining learner? Doesn't he just have to sit there and teach the same thing over and over again to the class failure, instead of learning something for himself? And worse, isn't this just asking learners to do the teacher's job? You may well get parents asking this and they deserve a response.

First of all, Cooperative Learning does not remove the teacher's responsibility to properly differentiate teaching, but it should be seen as one tool among many to achieve differentiation.

Second, as we have pointed out, Cooperative Learning does not replace individual work. Rather, it is a tool to ensure deep understanding and permits children to work successfully individually.

Third, all CLIPs integrate equal participation, which means that everyone has an equal right to speak and to be heard. This includes higher- as well as lower-attaining children.

Fourth, higher-attaining children may be very clever subject-wise but they may not be particularly adept at transferring their knowledge or selling their ideas. What good is a genius these days when hundreds of specialists are required to build even the simplest electronic gadget? The ability to communicate effectively and work with different types of people, including those less gifted than yourself, is a crucial skill.

Fifth, Cooperative Learning is much, much more than teaching something to someone else, just as it is so much more than partner talk. By explaining something to another person, you get the opportunity to revisit your knowledge and often find it wanting. You struggle to identify that subcomponent in your oh-so-brilliant exposition that your peer fails to grasp, you experiment with examples, you home in on his body language and facial expressions to see if you are getting warmer and if the bulb lights up. By deconstructing knowledge and skill sets to make conscious what before was simply intuition increases your ability to transfer your understanding to other tasks more effectively. And, let's be honest, does solving one more task on the board actually do that?

Finally, there is the social aspect. By making them contribute to successful learning, Cooperative Learning transforms high achievers' traditional role as sycophantic pariahs to highly valued partners and appreciated team members.

Children with SEND

SEND and Cooperative Learning really deserves a book in its own right. All Cooperative Learning activities adhere to rigid rules of engagement and time constraints in one form or another. For learners with ADHD symptoms, many CLIPs (including Catch1Partner) involve movement, with frequently changing partners and tasks, which allows them to let off steam normally built up to the point of explosion during endless sitting. The attention deficit element is usually triggered by non-action. If someone demands the attention of a child with ADHD by posing a direct question, there is a much higher chance of focused engagement.

For learners on the autistic spectrum (and that is a wide spectrum indeed), the lure lies in the absolute rigidity of the interaction itself. You know what you are supposed to be doing, when you are supposed to do it, with whom and for how long. Everybody follows the same rules, including rules on social behaviour. Especially in team-based Cooperative Learning activities you should be using a board timer anyway, but for someone with ASD, knowing down to the second when the activity will end makes all that human interaction endurable.

Finally, Cooperative Learning does not remove responsibility for supporting each child's personal development. While having autistic children participate in some Cooperative Learning activities may qualify as a big success, it should only be seen as a starting point. Cooperative Learning can present incredible openings to work with the unique needs of each child with SEN, without detracting from the quality or time allotted to the rest of the class. (Please also refer to the section 'What's in it for the SENCO?')

In summary, Cooperative Learning offers something positive for everyone by organising a space for every single individual to contribute to, and benefit from, others. This applies equally to children and adults.

Chapter 6

The Story of Stalham

A Reflection on Implementation Across a School

In the late afternoon of 26 November 2016, two Ofsted inspectors walked out of Stalham Academy. They had left the senior leadership team with a good judgement, the first for the institution under its many guises in 17 years and a huge change to the previous rating of inadequate. As it later turned out, the main reason it was not graded outstanding was the grossly inaccurate predictions of the visiting inspectors.

This is the story of how such a turnaround was achieved in the midst of the worst possible circumstances. At the heart of the solution-to-almost-everything-at-once was getting the approach to teaching and learning right.

Two years previously, on 30 April 2014, the school had the following issues:

+ It was in special measures (and had been since before Drew's arrival).

+ It was about to be force converted to academy status.

+ The number of children on the SEN register was increasing (contrary to the national trend); 19–25% over the previous three years.

By chance, two events had occurred within a few months of each other. First, Drew – through a bizarre interconnected network of mutual friends, the growing fad for communal events and the universe just deciding to give them a break – met Jakob. Jakob had opened his consultancy in the autumn of 2013 and was slowly realising that nobody seemed interested in his take on an inexpensive and simple solution to most of the problems everybody in education was (and still is) complaining about. From Drew's perspective, most of Jakob's blog posts at cooperativelearning.works were actually guides to how Cooperative Learning turns what are sometimes vague fad concepts into practical classroom action.

Running concurrently to this, Drew attended a 'How best to utilise your pupil premium money' seminar run by Norfolk County Council, where the results of the Sutton Trust and Education Endowment Foundation Toolkit were discussed (an interesting concept given that pupil premium money actually covered up cuts in funding). Here, collaborative learning was seen to offer a very good bang for your buck approach (+5 months of additional progress per learner per year on average).[1]

At this get-together, and already knowing something about the structural approach to Cooperative Learning from Jakob, Drew asked for clarification on what the Sutton Trust and Education Endowment Foundation meant by 'cooperative learning'. 'Group work' came the response from the course trainer.[2] 'We do lots of group work already and it doesn't work,' piped up a woman from somewhere behind him. 'It's too trendy and Ofsted don't like it,' said another, 'so I'm just going to get my teachers to read from a script.'

Knowing something, but not a great deal more than his discussions with Jakob, and trialling a Cooperative Learning approach with a few CLIPs since January 2014, Drew decided to keep quiet. He was acutely aware that opening any further discussion would meaninglessly add vital minutes on to the session when he needed to be back in school to teach after lunch. But Drew believed that a possible solution might have been found to many of the school's issues: a structured Cooperative Learning approach to classroom practice that could drive the school forward and be a tangible focus for the whole school.

Preparation – lining up your own ducks first

In the summer holidays of 2014, Jakob and Drew sat down and worked on matching Jakob's training programme to the desired outcomes for Stalham. Based on these discussions, Drew decided that, over three twilight continuing professional development (CPD) sessions starting in September 2014, they would introduce Cooperative Learning Interaction Patterns (CLIPs) to all members of staff.

Introducing such a strategy was a big gamble. For a start there was the concept of Cooperative Learning itself; it seemed to be too child-centred and at odds with the

---

1 Education Endowment Foundation, Collaborative Learning.
2 As we have pointed out, this is not actually true. 'Collaborative or cooperative learning is defined as learning tasks or activities where students work together in a group small enough for everyone to participate on a collective task that has been clearly assigned. Each student can then achieve his or her learning goal if and only if the other group members achieve theirs': https://educationendowmentfoundation.org.uk/evidence-summaries/teaching-learning-toolkit/collaborative-learning/technical-appendix. It goes to show the unhelpful conflation of Cooperative Learning with group work.

dictates from above,[3] which Drew just chose to ignore. Neither Drew nor Jakob wanted the training to be seen as anything other than an option or a series of tools to enable teachers to help learners verbalise their thought processes. The CPD was constructed in such a way that the CLIPs were demonstrated to the teachers by them actually doing the CLIPs. Essentially, Jakob modelled and imparted concepts about Cooperative Learning and then let the teachers use the very same activities to discuss their thoughts.

Implementation

Following each of Jakob's twilight sessions, Drew went to lessons and observed how the teachers taught. CLIPs were simply intended to be a tool to help improve teaching and learning in the school. Drew never demanded to see a CLIP. If a lesson was decent and didn't have it – then great. If learning happened without it – fantastic. If the children were engaged and their formative needs met – wonderful. Teachers may have had a CLIP recommended to them, but it would never be asked to be seen. What Drew did notice was that where CLIPs *were* being used, there was a real sense that learners' thought processes could be heard with greater clarity and teachers were able to respond to this.

Jakob had paid attention and tailored his CPD to concentrate on the needs of the school first and foremost. The first three CLIPs chosen for this assault on the sensibilities were Catch1Partner, Word-Round and Rotating Role Reading (all discussed in Appendix A). The latter CLIP was chosen because, not only were pupil premium reading scores below the national average at the end of Year 6, but, not surprisingly, so were the reading scores of all children. The first two CLIPs were picked because they encompass the very essence of the content-free, drop-straight-onto-anything-you-are-teaching-ethos that is at the heart of these approaches.

In the following January, Sage and Scribe, Simultaneous Write-Round and Three for Tea were introduced. The training concluded with Ping-Pong-Pairs, Think-Pair-Share, Timed Pairs and Team-Pair-Solo in the Easter (some of which are described in Appendix A). Further to these, the school added their own version of Meet in the Middle after the religious education lead attended Jakob's course 'Islam in RE' in November 2014.[4] The

---

3   You will notice in Stalham's 2016 Ofsted Report that the inspectors have put 'cooperative learning' in inverted commas on page 3: Ofsted, School Report: Stalham Academy (24–25 November 2016). Available at: https://files.ofsted.gov.uk/v1/file/2634323.

4   Always one for catchy names, Jakob's full title for this course was: 'Islam in RE: Religious Literacy and Controversy Through Enquiry'.

point being, of course, that once a school has comprehended and mastered the principles of Cooperative Learning, they can be applied to any CLIP. This is the main reason why this book focuses exclusively on the single, versatile CLIP Catch1Partner. Get your foundations right and the structure will hold.

Behaviour, not just for learning

One of the key factors in implementing CLIPs, and necessary for their success, will always be the behaviours of the children. What needed to change at Stalham was their understanding of the nauseating phrase 'behaviours for learning'. Prior to this, the school's behaviours for learning ideals reinforced the traditional and dominant teaching styles: 'I will listen to the teacher and answer questions' mixed with the classic drivel of 'trying harder' (instead of offering useful guidance; besides, who gets to say how hard someone is trying?) or 'I will concentrate on my work' (again, who gets to say what concentrate looks like outside the auspices of a fruit juice manufacturer?).

To mandate the change, Stalham's behaviours for learning statements were reduced to just four basic sentences, devoid of confusing modal verbs, to support the use of CLIPs in the classroom:

1. Look at the person who is talking (not just the teacher).
2. Respond when it is your turn.
3. Engage in the learning.
4. Ask relevant questions.

After a short half-term spike in school sanctions, such as lunchtime detentions (otherwise known as consequences), after three warnings (particularly for breaching the first three) behaviours in the classroom improved. Fewer and fewer consequences were distributed. One of the key comments that visitors make is how well behaved the children are.

Cooperative Learning integrates with and supports whatever systems you have decided on; you would not allow kids to bully each other in the corridors, so don't allow them to wilfully ignore peers who are responding to a question. At the end of the day, allowing such behaviour undermines the self-confidence of all parties concerned. While detention for not looking at the person speaking may sound harsh, it is simply a means to secure the outcomes for all children, including the sinner himself, who will benefit from such a basic social skill as eye contact for the rest of his life.[5]

Sustainability

Glenn Russell officially took up the position as head teacher in May 2015, one year after the trust's arrival and nine months into the development of Cooperative Learning at Stalham. Glenn has a 'degree in people' in much the same way that England cricket captain Mike Brearly was also renowned. He is also a great systems and community builder. In essence, he knew that the culture, ethos and development of the entire school community were reflected in the systems they used. At this point in time, the majority of teachers were utilising CLIPs but often not to their full potential.

Drew and Glenn looked at the CLIPs and saw them as tools. Aside from their other uses, these tools could be used effectively to develop teachers following 'observations'.[6] Peer support, in the form of collaborative action research approaches such as Learning Study or Three Way Views, were also utilised to help develop the effective addressing of concepts in maths through CLIPs. Following a standard lesson study model,[7] teachers not only began to see how the formative assessment system could be linked to planning, but also the role of themselves and their CLIPs to support planning and the children's learning in the long term. From this, a system for teaching evolved from the primordial soup of the first three CPD sessions.

Interestingly, after a time, teachers noticed that a pattern seemed to emerge almost organically in specific lessons, which became the pyramid model (see Figure 6.1). It must be noted that this was never enforced, dictated from above or expected to be seen. What evolved was, essentially, a Cooperative Learning session which fitted within the traditional hour-long period of a primary school day.

---

5 This applies to wilful disobedience only; children with SEN are a different story and are discussed in the section 'What's in it for your learners?' and at relevant points elsewhere. Suffice to say, children working in teams does not entail a robotic approach to the needs of individuals.
6 See Werdelin, Making Best Use of … Leadership; Coaching & Cooperative Learning.
7 That is, teachers work in threes to visit each other's lessons, plan and discuss what has been seen.

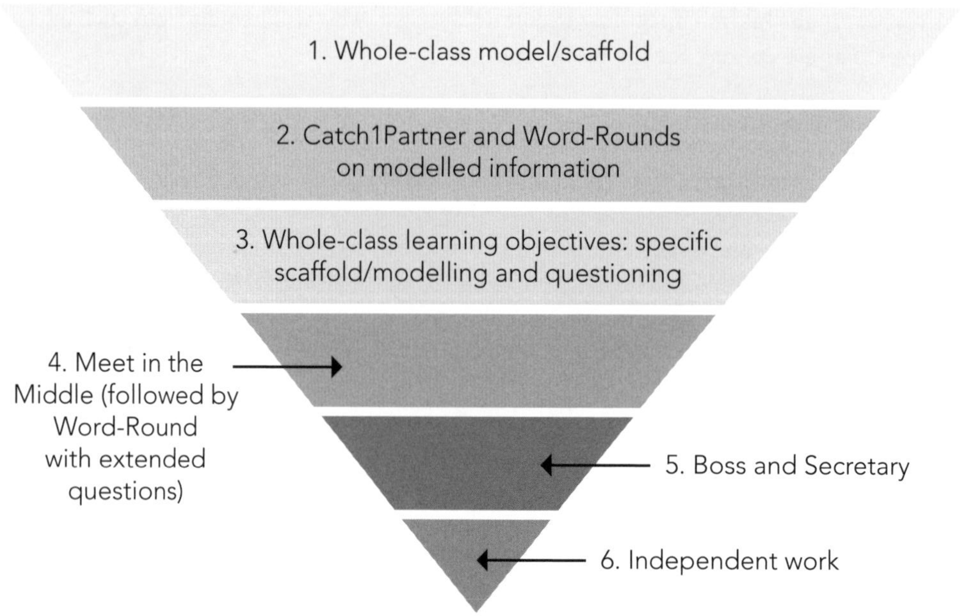

Figure 6.1. The pyramid model.

This pyramid works well for maths, some science knowledge lessons, grammar and MFL. (The astute reader will see here the outline of a Rosenshine lesson years before anyone in the UK had whispered his name.) The Catch1Partner at the start can be a revisited idea or the modelling of new skills for the session. That is up to the teacher.

Some important points:

+ As the six-part session progresses, the children work with fewer other students until each child is involved in individual work.

+ Teachers can remodel and adapt the model at any point.

+ It was not demanded that anyone had to follow this model.

This last point is extremely important because when visitors came calling following Stalham's endorsement by the Department for Education and asked to see Cooperative Learning in action, Drew and Glenn would look at the clock and could predict (especially if everyone was teaching maths at the same time) what they were likely to see. It just evolved that way. Looking back, what some guests might have taken away is that the pyramid system dictated what would be seen and when, and therefore we could hold teachers to account for any infractions by simply walking into a room. This was never the case at Stalham. The pyramid evolved to allow lessons to flow. It allowed children to move at their own pace with teachers listening to their thought process and following up misconceptions there and then.

In November 2016, Ofsted decided to grace Stalham with its presence. The inspection team that arrived did not believe the school was outstanding for a few reasons which are fully available in the Ofsted report. One bone of contention, which is not mentioned, was that they did not believe the school was 'on track' to meet national averages – which it had exceeded the previous year.[8] Still, they left the school with a good and everyone was happy. At this juncture, there is not much use in raking over the old ground of judgements, but when the results came in on that July morning the school had a combined (reading, writing and maths) score of 91% and 96% for those children who qualified for the pupil premium.

Stalham's story goes on. Staff and children continue to enjoy the success and the congeniality of the school's systems. It is a testament to how well-planned and considered school improvement can really turn a school around. The linchpin of that turnaround was adopting Cooperative Learning in spirit and practice across the board to support everything from behaviour policy to assessment systems, from staff meetings to parent get-togethers.

Beyond Stalham

Replicating Stalham's success is not impossible. As we began drafting this book, Henderson Green Primary Academy had just achieved 90% in their 2019 SATs after two years of concerted effort. The school, which had been labelled 'the worst school in Norfolk', had been bogged down in requires improvement since 2013, and in the previous two years had seen six people step in to lead the school before engaging with Cooperative Learning under the aegis of Adam Dabin. The school was graded good in November 2018.

Notably for a school of its ilk, the Ofsted report notes: 'There have been no exclusions this academic year.'[9] The school is located in a poverty-stricken area of Norwich with a long history of academic under-attainment and a multigenerational distrust for the educational

---

8   Ofsted, School Report: Stalham Academy.
9   Ofsted, School Report: Henderson Green Primary Academy (20–21 November 2016), p. 6. Available at: https://files.ofsted.gov.uk/v1/file/50049537.

establishment. When Jakob started working with him, Adam recounted his first impression of the school: 'It's in the middle of lesson time and suddenly this group of boys come hammering down the corridor on their scooters, shouting and banging on the glass panes and doors to the classes to get their mates to come join the fun – which they did. It was mayhem.'

The beauty of Cooperative Learning is that the development of social skills is fully integrated with academic achievement. There is no longer a discussion about giving priority to one over the other. Learning to calculate or read is intimately connected to getting along with other people. Children do not acquire tolerance or respect (or, indeed, character traits such as resilience) by being told about them or seeing them on an 'Our School Values' poster on the classroom wall. Rather, through Cooperative Learning, these vague concepts take on a concrete form which is built into the way children interact moment to moment, every day in every lesson. Social skills and noble values simply become a part of day-to-day teaching and learning. As a consequence, in the Cooperative Learning classroom many problems are dealt with proactively rather than reactively.

However, in schools such as Adam's you must start from scratch. You would not expect a child coming into Reception to have the ability to write or solve mathematical problems. The reason for this is that most children are not taught English and maths at home because there is an implicit understanding that this task rests with the school. Unfortunately, most children are not taught how to listen, how to follow instructions, how to respectfully engage other people, how to be patient or how to take turns at home either. This issue is not limited to the usual suspects – far from it. Wealthy academics are just as capable of cultivating unhelpful character traits in their children, and those children have just as much right to learn how to comport themselves in a positive way as those who might be more obviously short on social capital. Difficult learners don't need to be told what they mustn't do, but rather to have demonstrated and to practise every day what to do instead.

So, what to do with those children whose entire status in school is based on their bad reputation? This is where consistent team-building and class-building becomes important. One anecdote from Henderson Green serves to explain this. The children who were disruptive, violent or abusive were routinely removed to the intervention room across from their class. However, looking through the glass panes facing the corridor, they now saw their peers milling around in Cooperative Learning activities, laughing and smiling at each other. All of a sudden, the intervention room is no longer the cool place to be. As Adam explained, they are in a mind-boggling paradox because school is 'not supposed to be fun', according to generation upon generation of estate wisdom. Yet it is.

> Pupils want to come to school because they enjoy learning.
>
> Ofsted, School Report: Henderson Green Primary Academy[10]

Slowly, with unwavering, instant consequences to clearly defined behaviour breaches, but a no-hard-feelings-return-to-class policy, even the most difficult children, who had previously failed at absolutely everything the school required – from simple things such as sitting still on a chair to reading a sentence aloud – reintegrated into an invigorated learning environment. The crystal-clear guidelines and scaffolding, the increased activity levels and, especially, peers' positive expectations and willingness to help them were the main factors in this conversion. The term 'positive peer pressure' is an apt description for this process, where children regulate their behaviour in order to fit into the group. The social element in Cooperative Learning seems to leverage behaviour patterns on the deepest evolutionary level: without the tribe, you cannot exist. What would start with a stilted, shy, tentative or even aggressive, 'Thank you for helpin' me' soon makes authentic, positive behaviour seem as natural as breathing. With a sense of belonging, contributing and being valued comes the mental space to learn. Hence, the first iteration of Catch1Partner we looked at in this book is geared towards basic social skills.

10 Ofsted, School Report: Henderson Green Primary Academy, p. 6.

Chapter 7
Teaching Materials
The Stuff You Don't Need to Buy

In this chapter, we will look more closely at the inputs you can use in Catch1Partner, how to choose well and how these choices affect your outcomes.

Like all other Cooperative Learning Interaction Patterns (CLIPs), including such classics as Think-Pair-Share and Jigsaw, Catch1Partner requires you to add relevant content. You have seen that only by combining Catch1Partner with input such as flashcards do you turn the CLIP into an activity, but only by combining it with relevant input do you achieve your objective. Simply being active is not the same as the children learning what you are trying to teach them. Only by recognising relevant quality input will you and your children benefit from the full potential of the activity, so there is good reason to take a moment to reflect on the materials you are using with CLIPs.

Input here is defined not only as physical materials but also the questions and subtasks you are adding to the generic CLIP. For example, physical materials for Catch1Partner could be simple Q&A flashcards, but you might also insert a subtask (e.g. asking for an example from your peer) or a spur-of-the-moment inspiration during the activity for a question that you want discussed every time they meet with a new partner (e.g. 'Before you swap cards and move to the next partner, discuss how your two flashcards refer to our general topic on evolution' or 'Before you answer the main questions about decimal places, quickly compare your cards and decide which card has the greatest value').

Picking good materials

The first step to recognising good materials is to have a very clear idea of the outcome you want to achieve. For example, do you want to do rapid recall? If so, use flashcards with a question on the front and the answer on the back (Activity 2). Do you want the learners to have a reflective conversation about the book they are reading? If so, use cards with open questions: 'Who is the main character and how do you know?' 'Sum up the story until this point, please.' 'What do you think will happen in the next chapter?' (Activity 3). Try out the photocopy-ready flashcards in Appendix B or find an endless supply of free resources online.

Once this basic decision has been made, the next criterion is the simplicity of accessing and deploying the material, weighed against how much it will achieve in relation to your objective(s). Why spend hours searching online only to type out, print, photocopy and laminate a set of 32 full-colour hand-illustrated cards of open questions from a colleague on Pinterest (for a topic you will only revisit once a year!), when your objective only requires six to eight questions in black-and-white text? If you cannot be bothered to make the cards yourself, simply step into your class, write those eight questions on the white-board or flip chart, distribute responsibility for them to groups of children, give them 30 seconds to copy your questions onto scrap paper and you are ready for Catch1Partner.

It is important to reiterate here that there is no requirement for all the questions in a Catch1Partner to be different. As we have seen, there is no problem with learners seeing the same question over and over again because, thanks to the nature of Catch1Partner, they will be presenting and discussing them with different partners. Furthermore, having only eight crucial questions in a full-class card set means you won't need to revise as often as if you had eight crucial questions and 22 'filler' questions. Given the stress all educators find themselves under these days, everything boils down to achieving more with less. Cooperative Learning is one of the best ways to achieve high output for less input. Always think: how can I get the children to do more and me to do less?

Learner-produced teaching materials and motivation

Activity 5 gives a detailed guide to the basics of children's production: ample scaffolding, modelling, time to flesh out good materials before getting feedback and lots of monitoring. If you have run this activity a couple of times, most likely you have already tweaked and changed bits and pieces to match your specific objectives, your unique style as a teacher and your learners' particular needs. You have probably also wondered just how far you can take children's production.

Two important points here. First, only you can know where the current limits of each class are to be found. Second, whatever the limits, they should be expanded gradually in slow but steady steps. For example, would you miss out on this activity because of their sloppy handwriting, or would you take the opportunity to raise their standards? Fortunately, Cooperative Learning has a built-in mechanism to help you do just that.

Let's look at it from the children's perspective. Unlike regular class teaching, where days or even weeks can pass before your poor work is noted by the teacher in the margin of your crumpled, greasy jotter, the consequences come hard and fast in Cooperative Learning. The time lapse from scribbling some nonsense on your flashcard to the first (of many) peers telling you it *is* nonsense may be as little as 10 seconds. And, to add insult to injury, these people then start asking what you actually meant and offer suggestions which they expect you to note down along with their name. Soddin' do-gooders!

While disregarding the teacher's gently disappointed margin notes is easy, disregarding 20 minutes of humiliation as your exasperated peers try to pull you out of the dummy-hole you have dug yourself into is not. But what joy when you *do* make an effort and *do* manage to copy verbatim a scaffolded two-word sentence onto each side of your card in reasonably legible handwriting to see your classmates go, 'Wow, this is really good!' and then to join everyone else in the Hall of Fame (aka 'the plastic box where we keep the flashcards'). On a positive note, you are surrounded by people who want to discuss their worked examples with you and support your endeavour. In the Cooperative Learning classroom, positive interdependence means you are never left in the lurch.

Those readers who have already split their classes into small fixed teams and done consistent team-building might consider equating peer support with a single clear message: 'We will *not* let a member of (our) team present a substandard flashcard to the rest of the class.'

In conclusion, the key to successful learners' products in Catch1Partner is to make sure that:

+ The level required to produce the material is appropriately challenging.
+ The scaffolding is sufficient to eliminate any excuse for failing and most excuses for making basic mistakes.
+ Above all, to have unyieldingly high expectations: 'We will not stop this until you can all write a legible, three-word sentence on both sides of your flashcard and we can present a complete card set to the other classes.'

Examples of simple materials

The first rule when considering materials for CLIPs is to avoid overthinking it. Cooperative Learning should make your life simpler, not more complex. For that reason, materials for Catch1Partner do not have to be fancy flashcards.

For example, halfway through the children solving a set of tasks individually, ask them to get up, find a partner, compare answers and discuss differences. Monitor and give brief hints to learners as needed. When you sit them back down, ask everyone who disagreed about any answer to put their hand up. If nobody does, and you didn't pick up anything amiss when monitoring the activity, there is a good chance that everything is good. If many put their hands up, quickly elicit the task(s) that caused conflict. Micro-plenary as needed. Back to individual work.

Perhaps the children have written an opening paragraph for a horror story or a romantic poem instead. If so, get up, find a partner, read out and present your work and get feedback based on previous modelling with the necessary scaffolded language ('I chose this word because …', 'What I like most about your work is …' and so on) – just like you normally would.

Remember, it won't cost you anything to ask the children to write down peer feedback as you have seen demonstrated in some of the exemplary activities. Again, there is no need to overthink anything: if they wrote their poem in their jotters, they enter peer comments into the same jotters, keeping everything in one place.

Online materials

You are not the first teacher in the world to use flashcards or cards with open questions. Almost everything is available for free. Instagram and Pinterest are big with teachers who like to share their materials. If you are looking for a more organised approach, consider sites like www.goconqr.com, where you can tailor and share your own materials and tap into the work of millions of teachers and learners across the globe. Many producers of educational materials also produce flashcards. An instant hit is Collins' SATs and GCSE flashcards (referred to in Activity 2). Many popular off-the-shelf systems, from PiXL and

Memory to Chris Quigley's Geography Companion, include printable flashcards that are perfect for Catch1Partner.[1]

However, even if you have found materials online, it is only fitting that children (of an appropriate age) do at least some of the cutting out, laminating and so on. It's not as if you did years of training to sit and cut out bits of scrap paper, is it?

Mistakes and materials

When learners are making their own materials for Catch1Partner, ask them to do as much of the work as possible and continuously expand the scope of 'possible' as discussed above. However, no matter the level of scaffolding, there is always a risk that mistakes are made. This is all well and good if they are spotted before they go into general circulation. It is less good if convincing misconceptions spread exponentially. It is a sensible idea to have an open talk with learners about their responsibility to check and recheck their products, alone and with their peers, and to describe the crippling damage they will do to their classmates if they are sloppy. The message is: 'We are all responsible for each other in this classroom.' For the learners, responsibility means not spreading lazy misconceptions. For teachers, responsibility means levelling the tasks appropriately and providing all relevant scaffolding – just like you normally would – to maximise their chance of success, and for all adults in the room to monitor vigorously during production and activity.

There are many ways to scaffold and support to reduce mistakes during production. For example, ask learners to copy key terms and their definitions from course books or other materials onto their cards. Many worksheet-style materials and sample test papers (e.g. SATs busters) come with an answer key, so why not let the learners write the question on one side, work out the answer in their jotters and, finally, check the results using the key before adding the correct answer to the other side of their card? In maths, for example, consider how much of the calculation should be included on the back of the card along with the answer. Consider embedding hints along with the question. The opportunities are endless.

Again, you will find endless resources online. Combine science and ICT to browse the dictionaries of sites such as www.lovemyscience.com and convert information into cards. Here is the first word from the site's glossary: 'Absorbent – a substance that can soak up a

---

1   See https://www.pixl.org.uk, https://www.memory.com and https://www.chrisquigley.co.uk/product/new-curriculum-companion-geography.

liquid, or to take in energy and retain it.' Just remember that copying or even memorising information is not equal to actually understanding it. Rapid recall needs to be seen as one element in a larger scheme. However, endless repetition with very simple subtasks such as asking, 'Can you give me an example of something absorbent?' 'Uh, toilet paper?! (snicker, snicker)' goes a long way. They *will* remember it.

Imagine you are a science teacher and you've found the following definition of 'acid' online. Here is yet another chance to develop the children's cognitive and linguistic skills while you are producing materials that will benefit them for the next couple of decades.

An acid is a chemical that will neutralise an alkaline base, such as potassium hydroxide (KOH) or sodium hydroxide (NaOH). There are many different types of acid – for example, citric acid is a weak organic acid that forms naturally in citrus fruits and acetic acid in vinegar. Acid disolves in water to form a solution with a pH below 7. Acids contain hydrogen, which can be replaced by a metal to form a salt. $H^+(aq)$ ions are formed when an acid dissolves in water. Strong acids include hydochloric acid (HCl), sulphuric acid (H^2SO^4) and nitric acid (HNO^3). A commonly found weak acid is ethanoic acid (CH^3COOH).

The astute teacher will give this to a higher-attaining learner and ask her to decide which bits of this spiel are sufficiently relevant to fit onto her 5cm x 5cm card. Is there a simpler and more concise way to get the key points across? Furthermore, as is the case with the internet in general, anything found there has to be regarded with a certain suspicion. Can she spot the two spelling mistakes?

Note: Learners should sign and date every card they make. Accountability! Also remember that you or another staff member should give your stamp of approval before cards go into circulation.

Materials, Cooperative Learning and reducing your workload

The fact that Catch1Partner filters out a great deal of careless mistakes before you need to waste your time on them is a bonus, so regular Catch1Partner activities should not be seen as 'extra work'. In general, if you feel you are doing more work with Cooperative Learning, something is seriously wrong. Step back and reassess how you find your materials, how you are levelling tasks and, especially, how much work you are putting into scaffolding and staging the activities. Cut down on your ambitions. Aim for a 20:80 staging-to-activity ratio, then reduce to 10:90. For simple repeated activities, go for 2:98. Drew's record is a combined total of seven minutes of teacher talk in a 45 minute lesson, including the presentation of subject content and the staging of three or four different CLIPs. It can be done – and, most significantly, it can be done by you.

Chapter 8

The Pitfalls of Cooperative Learning

Things That Go 'Bump' in the Classroom

Nothing just runs by itself, and Cooperative Learning is no exception to this rule. In this chapter, you will find some common maladies and their cures.

Why Cooperative Learning fails on a school-wide level

Like all other initiatives to improve teaching and learning, Cooperative Learning is susceptible to leadership taking their eye off the ball. Stalham made do with nine hours of CPD to get 91% combined (reading, writing and maths) in SATs. But Jakob has worked with schools which did twice that amount and still found that Cooperative Learning had relatively little impact. The most common reason for this is not the staff. The problems are usually that the school leader:

1. Did not understand Cooperative Learning and its potential, while thinking that he did ('Ah, it's just advanced talk partners'), and therefore did not define a suitably ambitious vision. Nor did he set clear expectations for staff, leaving individual teachers to handle a haphazard, uncoordinated deployment which all too soon dissipated.

2. Understood what he bought, defined a vision and set clear expectations, but failed to allocate the resources to support the follow-up: implementation, sharing good practice and interlacing with data tracking, performance management, other professional development initiatives and his school improvement and development plan.

3. Got (1) and (2) right, but then didn't put suitable members of the leadership team in charge of the follow-up process.

4. Got all of the above items right, only to get sidetracked by an impending Ofsted inspection, academisation or the sudden loss of key staff, instead of considering how Cooperative Learning could help him to weather the storm. Cooperative Learning can tick Ofsted's boxes, it can prove the new MAT does not have to fire the leadership team, and it can make the induction of new staff easy by virtue of its simplicity. (As Drew says, reminiscent of famous American football coach Mike McCoy, *This* is how we play.)

Why CLIPs fail in classrooms

There are some common causes to why CLIPs fail to be implemented effectively within individual lessons. Here are the top three reasons that are either perceived to be a barrier or cited as a reason for Cooperative Learning not working.

1. The CLIP substitutes for any independent work

This is the simplest to explain: the CLIP leads to independent work and not the other way around. This goes back to Rosenshine's principles (described in Chapter 3) and the fact that guided practice should precede independent practice. The purpose of posing ideas, challenging, making links and bringing forth your inner voice is to help provide a template for the thought processes that will support the learning and facilitate independent work. If we recall the Teaching and Learning Cycle in Chapter 4, the joint construction supports and builds on modelling and language to aid the independent work which invariably follows. For example, in Key Stage 1–3 maths, much attention has been paid to the use of reasoning sentence stems. These sentence stems embody the concept of developing inner thought processes. CLIPs support this because they provide a pattern through which the sentence stems can be practised. Then, in any independent work, the sentence stems can be drawn upon to aid coherence and understanding.

2. Our learners are so different …

Or, our learners won't cope with the CLIPs, don't like talking, can't speak and so on. Blaming the children is always a way of putting up barriers in education. A choice needs to be made: if you don't want to apply Cooperative Learning, or staff don't want to do it, then don't do it. It's that simple. However, the learners take to CLIPs and get used to the repetitive comfort of the patterns much faster than the teachers. The pattern itself, as mentioned earlier, gives a consistency of approach that they appreciate. Yes, there are children who won't engage at first. They will in time. Will it be perfect straight away? No, nothing is.

The decision about how to unblock your drains and overcome barriers is really up to your style, although Stalham found that integrating the school systems to support CLIPs and joint construction was vital to its success. As for the 'our learners are so different', this has been heard by scores of people from advanced skills teachers, specialist leaders of education and local leaders of education to consultants and a myriad of other people who walk into schools on a regular basis. But if all the learners are so different, doesn't that mean they are all the same?

3. I need to let them 'have a go first' before I, as a teacher, intervene

This is a tricky one, and again it comes down to the pedagogical approach of your school. You can let the learners have a go at any content you put into the CLIP based on your prior knowledge of what they are able to achieve; perhaps, through questioning, they will be able to participate in the learning. It's a technique that can be successful if the students' developed inner voices are strong. However, if the learners' inner voices are not strong then it is likely to be a waste of time. As new knowledge and vocabulary often requires introduction and modelling by the teacher, it is wise to be instructional and then to open up the discussion to pupils using the CLIP as a vehicle.

Someone once gave the analogy of a kite: sometimes you keep it close. Sometimes you let it go. Sometimes it gets stuck in a tree. Sometimes you tie a key to it during a thunderstorm. Sometimes it is made of cheese. If you wish to let the learners have a go first, then let them try out a CLIP – although if they will encounter or are required to use new vocabulary, then tell them about it first. As far as evidence-based best practice is concerned, refer to Chapter 3.

Common questions from teachers

Below are some questions that are often asked by teachers regarding the specific challenges of implementing Catch1Partner.

How do you deal with a child who doesn't want to speak?

The short answer is: in the same way you would deal with a child who refused to carry out any other task, such as filling out a worksheet or putting away writing materials. Aside from following your school's general procedures for disruptive or off-task behaviour, such lack of care for classmates should be tied in with appropriate school values (e.g. respect, resilience, helpfulness). These are not simply phrases on the wall that we memorise but things we do in practice. To stay silent when your peers' learning depends on your contribution is against everything a positive learning environment should be. We might ask: 'How would you feel if someone refused to speak to you?', 'What should we do if someone asks for our help?', 'Is this the way we behave in our class?'

This assumes that the child is making a deliberate decision not to speak because he cannot be bothered or doesn't like the partner with whom he has wound up. If the child has genuine SEN issues that stop him from interacting with other learners (and only you and/or your SENCO can make this assessment), make sure that you give him the tools he needs to get involved and make sure that his classmates get the tools they need to accommodate him, even if it is accepting that he has special 'rights'. Tie all this in with respecting diversity and disability, which are both obligations in the PSHE curriculum.

One school Jakob worked with was introducing Catch1Partner in a class with a very anxious boy (let's call him George) who was diagnosed with ASD. George flatly refused to stand up, move around and, especially, to let go of his flashcard; the mate tugging at his card would literally bring on a panic attack. Instead of giving up and parking him in a corner to fill out a worksheet, the teacher drew up a special set of rules for him, which were made clear to his peers. He was allowed to sit on a chair (with the other children responsible for walking up to him and checking regularly if he was available) and keep his flashcard. After some weeks, he was able to stand up. After some more weeks, he was able to swap cards without a meltdown. After more weeks, he was able to circulate on the periphery.

How do you ensure children's answers are correct with self-generated Q&A cards?

There are a number of ways to do this:

+ Carefully stage and model the production of materials.
+ (Possibly) provide answer keys.
+ Remind children of the skills necessary to filter basic errors (e.g. number sense in maths).
+ Monitor as materials are produced in advance of the activity.
+ Team-check everything in suitable CLIPs – Word-Round (described in Appendix A) is very useful here.
+ Monitor as materials are presented during the activity.

Please also refer to Activity 5 on integrating learners' products.

How do you ensure children's answers are correct in Catch1Partner?

By allowing learners to discuss and negotiate, you are generating visible learning for assessment (hopefully leading to assessment for learning), training vocabulary and creating as many opportunities for differentiated discussions as there are materials and possible pairs in the classroom. Against this is the risk of learners spreading misconceptions.

There are numerous safety measures for tackling this problem, which we have covered in previous chapters. Here is a summary:

+ Diligent explanation of concepts and detailed modelling of the application.
+ Where possible, working within a sharply delineated area when introducing anything new.
+ Modelling potential mistakes, their identifiers and their solutions.
+ Provide scaffolding, e.g. worked examples, vocabulary, sentence stems visible throughout the activity.
+ Providing simple tools to recognise blunders – for example, 'When adding even numbers, we know the result can never be an uneven number' (which is an opportunity to train number sense with no further work).

- Painstaking monitoring as the activity progresses and consciously choosing target children.

- Inserting written elements where expedient to curb quick and thoughtless oral conclusions and to add a visual assessment tool (simply look over their shoulders).

- Looking out for pairs who seem bogged down or involved in vitriolic discussions about subject content (if only!).

- Employing after-activity check-ups: 'Who disagreed?', 'What happened?', 'What did you conclude?'

How do you store Catch1Partner materials for later retrieval practice?

Every school organises their Catch1Partner card repository differently, but here are a few suggestions. You will need to find the way that works best for you.

- Get everyone on board. Priority should be given to producing materials that benefit the largest numbers of teachers and learners as often as possible. If all colleagues recognise the value of the materials, they are a great deal more likely to produce and log materials themselves.

- Make sure there is a consistent system for storing materials. For example, in a big multi-form entry school where you cannot pop in and out of classrooms, store them in the staffroom or wherever you normally keep teaching materials.

- Organise them by subject key stage or year right from the start. Add further granulation as needed. Consider coding by colour (e.g. red for English, purple for art) or shapes (square for Key Stage 1, rectangular for Key Stage 2), but don't forget the balance of simple production time against later ease of access.

- Ideally, materials that are used all the time should be laminated (why redo your shredded cards after three months of wear and tear?). Laminating also confers a sense of importance and value, especially when materials are produced by the learners.

- Keep a logbook/inventory next to the materials (just like the library). Which teacher/class added what when, and – especially – who took out cards and did not put them back? If you run the inventory on a suitable digital platform, you have the benefit of adding tags that can be searched for and cross-referenced (e.g. #maths, #SAT, #fractions).

Consider allocating responsibility for the repository to a dedicated staff member who will make sure that everything is put away in the correct place, properly logged and everyone is aware of new additions. If you do Catch1Partner in every subject every day, after a full calendar year you will have a set of core materials in one place and a great deal of paraphernalia.

How do you deal with an odd number of learners?

The quick answer is: whatever you usually do for talk partners and the like. Here are some examples:

+ Create a 'pair' of Siamese twins out of two children: for the duration of the activity they act as one learner. Take the opportunity to train a struggling learner by joining her to a skilled 'guide' who can model interactions in detail and/or support subject knowledge and give suggestions and prompts when the lower-attaining pupil represents the twins.

+ Drop yourself or the TA into the role of a learner. This will provide lots of detailed learning opportunities for you as a teacher. (We strongly suggest you always keep at least one adult free to monitor the class as a whole.)

How do you ensure that one person does not dominate during the 'pair' part?

By rigorously following the steps in the CLIP, equal participation and positive interdependence is secured. This is the reason that we – save a few special occasions – never change the steps in the CLIP.[1] The steps in Catch1Partner require partner A to present a question and partner B to answer. If partner A is a timid, lower-attaining child, he or she may choose to sheepishly show the written question while staring at the floor. It is your responsibility as a teacher to model what partner B is supposed to do, which could be to prompt (in bold) partner A to speak her part:

Emma, could you **please read the question out to me** … **Louder please**, there is a bit of background noise … Thanks. **Really appreciate that**, I know you've said you sometimes feel shy. I think the answer to that question is … Is that correct? No, **don't show me the other side of the card, tell me**! I don't understand what you mean … Oh, I see … Well, maybe I wasn't being clear because I sort of meant the same thing.

....

1 In fact, the only exception in the present volume is cutting out step 6 in Catch1Partner (partners swap materials) in activities where the materials are only relevant to that person or the person has unique knowledge of the card, such as pronunciation allocated to individuals (e.g. the early stages of Ms Schmitt's German lesson in Activity 6).

Right, no, I see what you're saying – it's the vocabulary that's not precise. Thank you, couldn't have done it without you, Emma! Are you ready for my question?

How do you address a pair who do not move on?

Many learners prefer to stay in their comfort zone. This is one reason that at least one adult should monitor the whole class at any given time: step in quickly and gently nudge the procrastinating pairs. You likely know who to look out for.

How do you stop children rushing to their friends?

Strict rules should be in place at all times to approach only the closest free person regardless of who they are. On the rare occasions where there is a choice between two partners, priority should be given to the person they do not normally sit with.

How do you keep conversation focused on the task?

Most schools find that this is not the big problem you might expect it to be, but do monitor and challenge off-task behaviour as you would normally.

What do you do with the assessment information you glean?

The short answer is: do what you ordinarily would with assessment information. In general, make sure that the organising of any written evidence requires minimal work from you – for example, any peer feedback on a romantic poem goes straight into the same notebook as the original text.

How do you scaffold language?

Model it clearly and make sure it is always available for learners, whether on cards, the whiteboard, flip chart or posters.

How do you ensure the questioning challenges all children?

In Catch1Partner, the learner's responses will naturally create differentiation. For example, take the question: 'What do you know about the First World War?'

Partner A: They wore, like, you know, gas masks. And were dirty… uh, can you help?

Partner B: I know the First World War started in 1914 and involved many countries in Europe. I also know it's called the 'trench war' because they lived in trenches in France. And they had planes with two wings. On top of each other, like this *[mimics with hands]*.

You can add a metacognitive challenge to open questions by adding a subtask: 'Organise any answer into "I am certain that …" and "I think that …" when you respond' (and remember to clarify the difference before setting them off). You can also add a memory challenge by asking peers to list what their partner said just before the pair splits up.

As for flashcards with a closed question on the front and an answer on the back, you can present differentiated versions of the task on the same card and ask partners to pick their challenge level before posing the questions. Follow any system that you are currently using (e.g. chilli challenge). Never, ever, reinvent any wheels.

In every case, simple subtasks in the form of a fixed question (e.g. 'What else do you know?', 'Prove it to me!', 'How do you know?') does wonders for even the simplest questions.

How do you train the children to ask each other clarifying and probing questions in a positive manner?

Model. Monitor. Challenge. Every day. Every lesson. Until it is a given, like breathing. For some classes this is a matter of weeks, for others months. But it can and must be done. Consider using any current reward system: 'I heard Ahmed be very helpful to Yang-Lin. I'm going to give him a point for that! Well done, Ahmed!'

Chapter 9

Cooperative Learning and Other Strategies

One of the things many teachers like about Cooperative Learning is the fact that it is so non-competitive in terms of other teaching approaches. No matter what systems or schemes your school has invested in previously, you will not lose out by adopting Cooperative Learning. One obvious example is the comprehensive connection to Rosenshine's principles of instruction as delineated in Chapter 3. It is never either/or. Rather, in all the schools we have worked with as consultants or specialist leaders of education, we have yet to see a system that has not been enhanced by the intelligent deployment of Cooperative Learning.

In this chapter, we will briefly give a couple of examples of some common systems already in place in UK schools and explore how teachers and leaders we have worked with have successfully integrated them with Cooperative Learning. Aside from the cases listed, some of the successful examples of symbiosis we have seen include the much vaunted (but to many teachers slightly nebulous) metacognition, prescriptive recipes such as Read Write Inc., and classroom management techniques from gurus such as Sylvia Clarke and Doug Lemov. Read what is relevant to you and be creative.

The key to getting Cooperative Learning integration right is to understand how much room you have to manoeuvre without jeopardising the systems you are already using successfully (and/or in which you have invested an inordinate amount of money). The best approach is to look at the intended outcomes, materials and procedures that are essential to your system, and then deploy Cooperative Learning to support those outcomes and using those materials and procedures. Minimum amount of work is the name of the game.

> No matter what systems or schemes your school has invested in previously, you will not lose out by adopting Cooperative Learning. It is never either/or.

Lesson plans

Whether you have been issued with rigorously detailed plans, create your own or use templates such as Ross Morrison McGill's 5 Minute Lesson Plan, Cooperative Learning will support the various phases of your lesson. For example, modelling is one of the five factors required in Shaun Allison and Andy Tharby's Making Every Lesson Count series. You can simply integrate the conscious modelling of the skill you are teaching into the staging of the CLIP, as we have seen in previous chapters. No time is lost and it all fits together.

What happens if you have bought into a system that requires learners to sit in rows, quietly facing the teacher? Well, this is one of the reasons why we chose Catch1Partner to demonstrate Cooperative Learning in this book. Catch1Partner does not require you to organise teams, move the furniture or send out opposing or confusing messages to learners. The message is simple: when we sit down, this is how we teach and learn. When we do Catch1Partner, this is how we teach and learn. For most kids, Catch1Partner provides a welcome break from individual work and regular talk partners and serves to energise the class – aside from the other outcomes which cannot be achieved by teaching from the board, such as basic social skills, self-confidence, oracy and so on. Simply copy questions from your selected system onto cards and launch your Catch1Partner.

Talk for Writing

Jakob first became acquainted with Pie Corbett's Talk for Writing programme back in 2015 when he did his 'Better Reading and Writing with Cooperative Learning' seminars in the West Midlands.[1] The system is now so prevalent in primary schools that he often follows Corbett's lesson outline when teaching CLIPs specific to both reading and writing and to demonstrate in practice how well Cooperative Learning supports even quite subject-specific approaches to teaching.

What makes Talk for Writing interesting in the context of Cooperative Learning is that it is a fairly rigid and comprehensive system. For those unfamiliar with it, Talk for Writing

---

1 See J. Werdelin, Better (Talk4)Writing through Cooperative Learning, *cooperativelearning.works* (26 April 2014). Available at: https://cooperativelearning.works/2016/04/26/better-talk4writing-through-cooperative-learning/#more-4086.

organises learning to write into three stages: imitation, innovation and independent application. While Catch1Partner does not support literacy as directly as other CLIPs in the archive (some of which are so tailored to reading or writing that they cannot really be used for anything else – see Appendix A), it does a lot to secure the ancillary objectives necessary to write effectively.

The *imitation* phase requires a 'cold task to establish key features of model text/processes to focus on', which could be a Catch1Partner on relevant new vocabulary, sentence structures or points of grammar needed for the target writing. This 'involve[s] pupils saying the words and phrases in context'. As you move on towards the *innovation* stage, the children are asked to 'Read as a writer: Box-up structure & analyse ingredients' and then get up, notes in hand, to share and compare their thoughts. Similarly, they can '[Share] planning & writing & model how to talk about the ingredients'.[2]

You can gradually insert and scaffold increasingly complex reflections and commentary on peers' ideas to match objectives, learning styles and special needs with no extra work. Once the children move into the *independent application* stage – getting relevant feedback and being challenged on the precision of their language, the frequency of certain words and the consistency of tense – everything you are picking up during monitoring can be negotiated in micromanaged and neatly differentiated discussions in Catch1Partner.[3]

SOLO taxonomy

Among all the pedagogical approaches that can have their value multiplied by Cooperative Learning, one method stands out. Unlike Talk for Writing, this unique approach mirrors the all-encompassing scope of Cooperative Learning, and, like Cooperative Learning, it also needs an avatar to become incarnate in the classroom. This approach is, of course, SOLO taxonomy.

SOLO stands for the Structure of the Observed Learning Outcome. At its most basic, it organises learners' performance into five distinct levels of increasing structural complexity: pre-structural, uni-structural, multi-structural, relational level, extended abstract. This taxonomy not only makes it possible to identify learners' levels at any given time, but it also makes it possible to classify teacher input.

2   P. Corbett and J. Strong, The Talk for Writing Process (n.d.). Available at: http://www.talk4writing.co.uk/wp-content/uploads/2015/04/T4W-overview-expanded.pdf.
3   You will find several relevant articles at cooperativelearning.works (search for 'better reading and writing').

Despite their superficial simplicity, both SOLO and Cooperative Learning can be applied to anything, at any time, to achieve virtually any objective within their respective fields. Here are a few items on the SOLO can-do list: 'plan teaching', 'assess and guide learning in relation to both functional and declarative knowledge' and 'give proximate, hierarchical and explicit feedback, feed-forward and feed-up on learning'.[4] However, as we know, doing everything all at once is seldom successful. Hence, getting SOLO firmly embedded in your school can be a time-consuming uphill struggle to first get everyone's head around the underlying theory and then anchor practice consistently across all classrooms, especially on top of everything else you have to do.

In order to stand a chance of assessing learners' SOLO levels and maximise feedback to shift them up the taxonomy tree, you need to make all learning very explicit. Nothing generates more explicit learning than Cooperative Learning. Simply walking around in a class in the midst of any CLIP provides 20 times the information on learning than any teacher can reasonably process. As a consequence, concerns about cognitive load suddenly apply to the teacher too.

Happily, nothing organises and structures that information avalanche better than SOLO. When teachers need to identify levels at a glance/eavesdrop, it's far simpler than Bloom's taxonomy. By using SOLO to classify and organise, you tap more fully into the assessment potential of Cooperative Learning.

In short, Cooperative Learning provides the high volumes of realistic data that SOLO needs, while SOLO increases the precision, speed and scope of what you can do with the high volumes of realistic data provided by Cooperative Learning.

Oracy

Oracy can be so obvious that it goes unnoticed, like not seeing the wood for the trees. At its heart, Cooperative Learning is organised communication. The Education Endowment Foundation Toolkit rates oral language interventions at five months of additional progress per learner per year based on extensive research, and directly connects this approach to 'collaborative learning'. The Education Endowment Foundation also note an intimate

---

4   P. Hook, *First Steps with SOLO Taxonomy: Applying the Model in Your Classroom* (Invercargill: Essential Resources Educational Publishers, 2016), p. 11.

connection between oracy and literacy, which we have pointed out above in the section on Talk for Writing.[5]

In December 2020, the Oracy All-Party Parliamentary Group released an interim report which not only highlighted that young people have unequal access to opportunities that develop their oracy skills in schools in England, but also emphasised that, on average, pupils from poorer backgrounds have lower levels of language development than their peers, and that this language gap on entry to nursery school widens throughout their schooling. As a consequence of the close links between language development and academic outcomes, poorer children tend to perform less well in tests and exams.[6]

If your school understands the value of oracy – whether to boost exam results, improve social mobility or widen participation in higher education – and has invested in programmes such as Voice 21, Cooperative Learning is the obvious way to increase the volume and focus of the talking in every aspect of daily learning processes. This quote from the Voice 21 website might as well have been a description of what learners do in a Catch1Partner on any random Monday morning at Stalham and elsewhere, which is to 'develop and deepen their subject knowledge and understanding through talk in the classroom, which has been planned, designed, modelled, scaffolded and structured to enable them to learn the skills needed to talk effectively'.[7] On the same homepage, you will find Voice 21's 'Oracy Benchmarks' which at once support and are supported by Cooperative Learning, starting with number one: 'Opportunities for oracy are regular, purposeful, appropriately pitched.' Indeed, the same arguments for Cooperative Learning would apply to any other communication-based approach, such as Philosophy for Children.

The upshot is that Cooperative Learning offers a value increase (often reciprocal) to virtually any other programme or approach your school has adopted or wishes to adopt. Many schools we have worked with have had some dead four-digit investment in this or that programme which has been reinvigorated by fusing it with Cooperative Learning.

---

5   Education Endowment Foundation, Oral Language Interventions (20 September 2019). Available at: https://educationendowmentfoundation.org.uk/evidence-summaries/teaching-learning-toolkit/oral-language-interventions.
6   Oracy All-Party Parliamentary Group, *Speak for Change: Initial Findings and Recommendations from the Oracy All-Party Parliamentary Group Inquiry* (December 2020), p. 9. Available at: https://d5119182-bdac-43d5-be55-e817e7736e5b.filesusr.com/ugd/2c80ff_33e3208ce4dd4764b154682488c53ef7.pdf.
7   See https://voice21.org/oracy.

A Conclusion of Sorts

For too long education has been a hard place to work. Shifting sands, moving goalposts and many other changing metaphors have rained down upon us. But there is hope. The rising interest in an evidence-informed approach to education sheds ever more light on what facilitates learning most efficiently. Systematic research confirms the value of direct instruction, clear modelling, feedback and so on in the development of learners' knowledge, cognitive abilities and, crucially, their potential. More findings will come in due course.

What Cooperative Learning offers is an evidence-based vehicle to implement these current and future research findings without substantial changes to the day-to-day running of lessons. The immutable Cooperative Learning Interaction Patterns (CLIPs) help us, as teachers, to guide practice, hear and respond directly to our learners' thought processes, and allow them to learn while acquiring key life skills – all irrespective of the latest research, policy changes and refocused Ofsted inspection guidelines. With CLIPs, your foundations stay the same; only the objectives and content change.

The key to this success is consistent, high-quality deployment and ongoing refinement, day in and day out, of Cooperative Learning. In practice, this means the well-organised, metred roll-out of CLIPs: mastering one before introducing the next; getting every step right; gradually adding more advanced tasks; building oracy, metacognition and social skills as you move along. If you are adopting Cooperative Learning as a school-wide approach (and you really should), the responsibility for this process rests firmly on the shoulders of the leadership team: the correct allocation of time and resources, support, CPD, peer coaching – whatever is needed to get the job done. As for teachers, success requires a firm grip on the core principles of teaching: knowing your subject matter; crystal-clear staging; effective modelling of interaction and language; classroom management; monitoring; feedback; reviewing; and all the other elements whose intimate relation to Cooperative Learning we have discussed.

For teachers and leaders alike, success with Cooperative Learning also means thinking about how your current strategies, resources or systems could be enhanced by Cooperative Learning to reduce workload, strengthen current good practice and increase the value of any prior investments. This will not happen without you taking ownership, trusting yourself and having the courage to see challenges and opportunities, tackling one and seizing the other.

Most crucially, success entails not just individual ownership, but collective ownership. You should approach Cooperative Learning as a shared endeavour and involve all stakeholders (even parents) in the organic growth of a Cooperative Learning practice that facilitates your school's practical targets and ephemeral vision in your unique circumstances.

The bottom line is that, in the right setting, all people are in fact resourceful, motivated and synergistic. Cooperative Learning, as presented here, is a strong contender to provide that setting.

Appendix A

More CLIPs – a Tactical Toolkit

As promised, here is a collection of Cooperative Learning Interaction Patterns (CLIPs) used at Stalham and many other schools with whom we have worked. Our advice is that you make sure you fully master Catch1Partner, apply the four basic rules and are fully aware of how Cooperative Learning interlaces with Rosenshine's principles of instruction (as outlined in Chapter 3).

Although the following CLIPs work for pairs and teams, you should be able to extrapolate most of what you need in order to succeed from your understanding and experience of Catch1Partner (be sure to refer to the Cooperative Learning checklist in Appendix C – photocopy it and stick it to your desk!). To be clear, there are probably hundreds of similar such collections of action steps under a plethora of names. However, when you find some new pattern on the internet, always ask yourself: does it facilitate PIES (positive interdependence, individual accountability, equal participation and simultaneous interaction)?

> When you find some new pattern on the internet, always ask yourself: does it facilitate PIES?

Please be aware that we are barely scraping the surface of the opportunities that these CLIPs offer (they really warrant a full chapter each), especially the topic of team-building and using teams as miniature safe zones for building character traits such as patience, helpfulness, communal responsibility and trust, while strengthening oracy warrants a multi-volume book in its own right.

The first CLIP presented here, the humble Word-Round, is the foundational CLIP in Jakob's work with the Higher Education Progression Partnership in South Yorkshire, where it operationalises the rather academic concept of 'possible selves' to build self-confidence and resilience and to draft alternative life narratives among those at risk of missing out on higher education opportunities.[1]

---

1   J. Werdelin, Widening Participation; How Cooperative Learning Can Put Possible Selves into Practice, *cooperativelearning.works* (27 October 2019). Available at: https://cooperativelearning.works/2019/10/27/widening-participation-how-cooperative-learning-can-put-possible-selves-into-practice.

A note on teams

Teams are ideally composed of four learners, with teams of three only when dictated by class size. These teams should stay together for four to six weeks, which is long enough to learn how to tackle fellow team members' idiosyncrasies but not long enough to get bored with one another. As a teacher, you (and only you) set up the teams; we suggest that you mix weak, strong and two mediums. Place them in pairs facing each other, with their side to the whiteboard so they can all see without craning their necks, and so you have a clear line of sight down each table from the front of the class. Assign a name to each of the four seats across the teams, so you can remote control all tables with a single command. For example, when you say: 'Person 1/Green Person/Giraffe, you have 20 seconds to get the materials for your team,' the learner in that seat from each team gets up and picks up the materials.

Word-Round

Learners are seated in teams of four (with one or two teams of three as dictated by class size).

The action steps are as follows:

1. The teacher presents a task with several possible answers.

2. Each person takes turns presenting an answer or solution to his/her team (usually limited by a timeframe or a set sentence limit).

The teacher usually asks for a consensus or individual response from selected tables.

The Word-Round is a great CLIP when you would like learners to explain their reasoning, but it can also be used to brainstorm, present work, drill times tables/months/ordinal numbers or simply to recap teacher input (reviewing, remember?). In terms of its flexibility and wide scope, Word-Round is the seated version of Catch1Partner, which is a daily workhorse in schools where Cooperative Learning is adopted seriously.

To enforce equal participation, limit the amount of input each learner may give during his turn. You can do this by restricting answers to a single sentence or two, but many teachers prefer timing turns (e.g. 15 seconds per person). There are lots of free loop timers online that you can display on your interactive whiteboard. A timer that produces a loud sound when each turn ends is preferable, as it means the teacher can keep her mind on the monitoring. The amount of time that learners have to respond is entirely up to you, but you should take into account the age of the learners and the question being asked. For a rough rule of thumb on the amount of time to give each person in the Word-Round, model the ideal answer to the question you have posed yourself, then add 10 seconds. In this way, you will be able to take into account the inevitable 'err' that starts each activity. Make sure that Word-Rounds always go the same way (either clockwise or anticlockwise) or they will quickly wind up in unnecessary discussions about whose turn it is.

To help you appreciate the scope of complex learning this superficially simple CLIP can facilitate, we have included a transcript from a Year 5 maths lesson in Appendix F. In it, you will find references to the hand signals used at Stalham, which learners use to give silent and unobtrusive feedback during their team members' presentation.

Meet in the Middle

Learners are seated in teams of a maximum of four.

The action steps are as follows:

1.   Each team is issued with the relevant materials.*

2.   The teacher presents a task.

3.   Each team member individually writes his/her own solution.

4.   Team members present their solutions in a Word-Round.

5.   The team discuss and write a communal solution (possibly negotiating formulations).

* This CLIP requires something to write on. There are endless variations but the simplest approach is to use their regular notebooks in step 3 and one A4 or A3 sheet of paper placed in the middle of the table for step 5.

Make sure your learners have fully mastered the Word-Round before you proceed with this CLIP. In Meet in the Middle, team members get the opportunity to think and formulate their own written answers, are prompted to uncover their own understanding in order to find common ground with their peers and reach agreement through discussion and compromise. Each team ends up with a finished product which, when evaluated against individual output in step 3, gives evidence of each learner's process of moving towards consensus.

Rotating Role Reading

All learners, seated in teams of no bigger than four, are each given a copy of some reading materials.

This CLIP is distinguished by having four or more roles. In its base form, these are reader, summariser, header and connector, but you can change or add depending on your learning objectives.

The action steps are as follows:

1. Person 1 reads a paragraph/sentence/specified extract to the team.

2. Person 2 summarises what has been read.

3. Person 3 headlines the paragraph (this clarification is best done in a short phrase).

4. Person 4 connects to the previous paragraph (or, if starting, predict what will happen).

5. The roles shift, so person 2 now reads the next paragraph/section, person 3 summarises and so on.

Rotating Role Reading is a fantastic CLIP to engage learners with reading and blend in some key comprehension strategies. It is also extremely flexible as you can add your own roles, such as person 4 answering a comprehension question from a list of questions provided by the teacher. Note that teams of three can dispense with step 5, as the roles in teams of four move along by themselves (i.e. person 1 reads, person 2 summarises, person 3 formulates a heading, person 1 connects, person 2 reads and so on). This CLIP requires a lot of confidence and resilience, so make sure your learners have fully mastered Word-Round first.

Sage and Scribe

This CLIP works in pairs. The teacher explains/demonstrates how to solve a procedural task step by step and, as always, leaves the full worked example(s) visible. Similar tasks are then presented to the learners (e.g. on the board or on worksheets).

Each pair should determine their roles: one learner is the Sage and the other is the Scribe.

The action steps are as follows:

1. The Sage orally repeats the step-by-step instructions on how to solve the task, one step at a time.
2. The Scribe follows these instructions step by step, asking coaching and clarifying questions if necessary.
3. The Scribe praises the Sage and vice versa.
4. Partners switch roles for the next problem.

Sage and Scribe (also known as Boss and Secretary) is ideal for mastering any procedural task – from setting up a science experiment to solving a maths problem. It is Rosenshine's dream because it directly emulates the teacher's modelling, and paradise for cognitive load fanatics because it breaks down complex procedures into small steps. In the bigger scheme of things, much of life is about procedures, from mathematical formulas to regular verb conjugations, following a cooking recipe to starting a car, assembling an IKEA closet to using a defibrillator. This CLIP encourages directional and procedural thought processes to be honed and developed. Careful attention should be paid to classroom pairings, the modelling of socially acceptable language when issuing commands or asking questions and, of course, the step-by-step clarity of the direct instruction.

Ping-Pong-Pairs

The action steps are as follows:

1. The teacher presents a task with several possible answers (usually with set parameters and based on previously taught knowledge).
2. In pairs, partners take turns giving their input.

Ping-Pong-Pairs is a deliciously short and fun CLIP which is brilliant for revision. It gets learners ready for learning and engages them in the use of concepts with which they need to be confident. For example, the task might be counting in multiples or listing consonants, adjectives or verbs in another language. Ping-Pong Pairs is a PIES-compliant alternative to talk partners and is faster to stage than Word-Round for tasks with ultra-short input. If your learners are in teams of four, place them in two pairs facing each other and vary Ping-Pong-Pairs between the front and side partner. Again, make absolutely sure that the learners have the scaffolding they need in order to succeed. If you are asking them to take turns listing the days of the week in Spanish, for instance, make sure there is a big fat poster they can glance at if they get lost. A snappy sense of mastery is what makes Ping-Pong-Pairs a success.

Sample Flashcards

You can copy these flashcards or download and print them from: https://drive. google.com/drive/folders/1aqfQGiV7VLEMF2NoivlwtUdk1Xe-0uu2 (https://bit.ly/ TheBeginnersGuideDownloads).

Key Stage 2–3: Class-building

What would be a perfect afternoon for you?	Where would you like to live – in the ocean or on the moon? Why?	If you had the chance to transport yourself anywhere, where would you go and why?	Have you ever had anything stolen from you? What was it?
What is one of your favourite things about a family member? Explain.	What magical power would you most like to possess?	If you had to give up a favourite food, what would it be and why?	If you were a flavoured ice cream, which one would you like to be and why?

How will life be different in 50 years' time?	What are your favourite hobbies? Why?	What can you do for hours?	What do you love about summer? What don't you love?
Is it better to read, watch TV or surf the net?	Who do you consider your hero?	Which animal would you prefer to be and why?	Which food would you like to eat endlessly?
Would you like to be a teacher? Why/why not?	What would make our class happier?	What can you do to make our class happier?	Do you like this activity? Why/why not?
What is the most exciting thing that has happened to you recently?	Have you praised an adult today? What made you do it?	Where in the world would you most like to visit? Why?	What do you have in common with everyone in your class?

What skill have you learned most recently? How did it feel?	Would you like to become a better reader? Why?	Who would you like to be other than yourself? Why?	Are our eyes the same colour?
What would be good/bad about being an adult?	Why is it important to be polite?	How can you show people you are listening?	What is your favourite music? Why?
Tell me about a personal interest you have or used to have.	Would you consider becoming a politician? Why/why not?	What profession would you not like to be in and why?	Is making money important to you? Why? If so, how do you plan to get some?

Key Stage 2–3: During/after reading a story/play

Who is the main character in the story? Do you like him/her? Why?	Where does the story take place? What is the place like?	When does the story take place? How do you know?
Is there an unkind character in the story? Who is it? How do you know he/she is unkind?	Does the main character have a friend? Why/why not? How important is the friend in the story?	Does the main character have any family? Why/why not? How important is the family in the story?
What is the best thing that happens in the story? Why do you like it?	What is the worst thing that happens in the story? Why don't you like it?	Do you think the story will have a happy ending? Why/why not?
Do you know anyone like the main character? How are they alike?	Do you think this book could be part of a series? Why/why not?	Could this story happen in real life? Why do you think that?

Is there a scary part of the story? If so, which part?	Do you like the story? Why/why not?	Have you read any other books by the same author? What were they like?
Is there anything in the story you didn't believe? If so, why?	What does the main character look like? Does it tell you or did you just imagine? Give some examples.	Are there pictures in the book? Describe some. Do they help you to read it?
Have you read the back cover blurb? Did it make you want to read the book? Why/why not?	Do you like the cover? Did it make you want to read the book? Why/why not?	Have you learned anything interesting from the book? What did you learn?
Is there an argument in the book? Who argued? About what?	Is there a sad part of the story? Why did it make you feel sad?	Does anyone lie in the story? If so, what was the lie?
Is anyone naughty in the story? What did he/she do?	Did anyone make a mistake in the story? What should he/she have done?	Would you recommend this book to anyone else? To whom would you recommend it? Why?

Would the story make a good film? Why/why not?	Would you read this book again? Why/why not?	Does the main character change in this book? If so, how?
Did any of the characters or events remind you of yourself? How?	Pick a random character. How did this character's actions affect you? Explain.	If you were the main character, how would the story change?
What surprised or confused you about the characters or events? Explain.	Which character do you think the author most sympathises with? Why?	What do you think the author is trying to accomplish?
How is the author thinking about the world?	How would the story change if presented from another character's point of view?	Do you think this story could actually happen? Why/why not?
How can this story teach us something about our lives?	How do you think the characters resolved the major conflict in the story?	How would you have resolved the major conflict in the story?

Key Stage 2–4: Metacognitive questions following the presentation of a solution (with worked examples) to a procedural task

Does anything in this presentation conflict with your prior understanding? Please elaborate.	How does this presentation relate to what you have learned already?	What questions will you be asking yourself next time you are working out this type of problem?
What is confusing about this topic?	What do you need to find out or do to get started on this type of task?	What method are you going to use for this type of task? Why?
Describe one strategy demonstrated that you found especially helpful.	Which materials are necessary/might help with this type of task?	Could there be a quicker way of doing this type of task? Explain.
Can you describe the problem in your own words?	Is there something in the presentation that wasn't clear to you? Maybe I can help …	Do you see any patterns or rules here? Please elaborate.

Can you think of another method that might have worked?	What have you learned or found out today?	Could any elements of this presentation be applied to other problems/tasks?
What new or key vocabulary was used in this presentation?	Does anything in this presentation confirm your prior understanding? Please give some examples.	Which of the worked examples made most sense to you and why?
What other problems fit this style or example?	Please can you list for me the steps to solve this type of task.	

Cooperative Learning Checklist

1. Do my learners know why they are using the Cooperative Learning Interaction Pattern (CLIP)?

2. Is the subject content relatively simple the first couple of times the CLIP is deployed?

3. Did I properly model the exact task they need to undertake in the CLIP?

4. Are my instructions clear? Did I use appropriate instruction-checking questions?

5. Are relevant instructions/support visible or otherwise available to the learners (on butcher paper, handouts or the whiteboard)?

6. Is the CLIP suitable for the task/question/objective?

7. Did I properly demonstrate and model the CLIP in front of the learners?

8. Is the timeframe reasonable? (It's better to give less time rather than too much. A lot can happen in a CLIP in a few minutes and you can always assign more time.)

9. Have relevant social skills been integrated into the CLIP and are they being used by learners? Did I model these skills appropriately?

For more inspiration, hints and ideas, please visit https://cooperativelearning.works.

Appendix D

CLIP Reflection and Coaching Guide and Assessment Guide for Teachers and TAs

The CLIP reflection and coaching guide for teachers and TAs and the associated assessment guide have formed part and parcel of much of Jakob's in-school training since 2014. In brief, the pre-activity reflection and coaching guide helps the teacher (or the TA doing the intervention) make decisions on specific areas relevant to planning a Cooperative Learning activity, and the post-activity assessment guide supports evaluation of the activity. Both guides form an excellent sounding board for personal reflection during planning and self-assessment, as well as a point of departure for coaching and professional development with colleagues to get the most out of any investment in Cooperative Learning (you will recall that peer support in the form of Learning Study was a part of Stalham's success story). Obviously, seeing their teachers collaborating and learning from one another also sets a good example for their learners.

The purpose of the pre-activity guide is to direct your attention to the areas where you need to make decisions in order to maximise the benefit of Cooperative Learning, while also simplifying your life as a teacher. Many teachers have found that filling out one or two of these in the early stages of launching a new type of activity is very useful. After that, use it as needed, especially prior to coaching sessions with colleagues and leaders.

Note: Under no circumstances should teachers be required to fill out this guide every time they want to do a CLIP.

The first two rows allow you to keep track of the formalities: jotting down how many times you have done a specific Cooperative Learning Interaction Pattern (CLIP) will help you evaluate your progress later.

The third row (Maximum time to spend on this CLIP …) is hopefully a reminder that Cooperative Learning takes up only as much lesson time as you want it to. Cooperative Learning should not take up the whole lesson; it does not even have to be done in every lesson. The CLIP should only occupy the time and space that you deem appropriate to achieve your objectives – whatever they may be – based on your experience, your personality, your pupils, your materials and your teaching style.

The first field asks you to define your objective (What do I want?). The more precisely you can define this intended outcome, the clearer your thinking. The next field (What is the content?) underlines that a Cooperative Learning activity is made up of the combination of a CLIP and some content. Remember, you should not need to generate lots of materials for Cooperative Learning activities. The opposite is the case, as indicated by the descending order of the tick boxes. (However, as we have discussed elsewhere in this book, any materials you do make can be reused almost indefinitely thanks to the possibility of adding subtasks.)

The next question (How should they behave?) emphasises that subject content and social skills go hand in hand, and this is true for every age group. It works both ways: Cooperative Learning requires basic skills such as turn-taking and active listening – skills that children do not always acquire at home. Nevertheless, we believe that these skills fall under the rubric of 'being prepared for life in modern Britain'. In secondary schools and colleges, especially, collaboration is a non-negotiable requirement in preparation for university or work. Finally, if you have a very challenging class or specific special needs pupils, remembering with which other staff members you have consulted might be very useful.

In the final part (How do I present CLIP instructions?), we have noted in detail the importance of careful scaffolding. Pausing to reflect on how to present instructions and ensure learners have access to relevant support materials are as relevant in Cooperative Learning as in individual work, perhaps more so.

As you can see, the guide lends itself to individual use. However, each section asks a leading question. If you choose to use the guide for coaching, these will be questions you are exploring with your coachee; simply add a 'why' and 'how' (e.g. Why did you choose this content instead of that content?) to allow your colleague to unpick each one. Try not to overthink the coaching, but see it as a chance to explore. The coach does not need to have the answers. The assessment guide simply covers the same themes retrospectively: what actually happened? How did reality hold up against the intended plan? What can we learn from this?

CLIP reflection and coaching guide for teachers and TAs (pre-activity)

TEACHER/TA NAME:_____ CLIP NAME: _____

Date:	Subject:	Whole class or subsets/interventions? _____
Class:	Lesson plan no.:	How many times have I done the CLIP now? _____

Maximum time to spend on this CLIP, including instructions: _____ minutes

What do I want? By the end of this CLIP I/my learners will have achieved this/these objective(s): • In support of my lesson plan: • Secondary objectives I would like to add or which will come about naturally through the CLIP:	**What is the content?** I used the following materials/oral questions/etc.: • I got away with using materials to hand. ☺ • I reused tailored material from another context/teacher. • I prepared special materials only with the CLIP in mind.

How should they behave?	How do I present CLIP instructions?
Social skills I think will be relevant/I want to promote:	• Orally. • Demonstrated with learner/team. • Whiteboard (on the fly). • Whiteboard (prepared slides). • Posters. • Student handouts.
Which phrases do I want them to use?	Do I need special instruction-checking questions, aside from those in my CPD handouts? Which ones:
I have sought help from a behaviour team member:	

CLIP assessment guide for teachers (post-activity)

Time actually spent on CLIP, including instructions: ____minutes

Were my objectives achieved? Why/why not? 1. From my lesson plan: 2. My secondary objectives:	How did my content work? Regarding materials, I have learned that:
How did my social skills foresight work? Which other social skills were actually needed? Is this an ongoing issue with this class that warrants further attention?	How did I actually present CLIP instructions? • Orally. • Demonstrated with learner/team. • Whiteboard (on the fly). • Whiteboard (prepared slides). • Posters. • Student handouts. • Instruction-checking questions.

From *The Beginner's Guide to Cooperative Learning* © Jakob Werdelin and Drew Howard, 2021

Next time:

What went well?

Any ideas for improvement?

Appendix E

Quick Reference

CLIP

CLIP is an acronym for Cooperative Learning Interaction Pattern. Our definition of a CLIP is a content-free series of action steps, pre-organised to let the teacher micromanage how learners interact with each other and their materials in such a way that, as a minimum, PIES are always promoted.

PIES

PIES is an acronym for positive interdependence, individual accountability, equal participation and simultaneous interaction. These four elements are the absolute minimum that a CLIP between peers must facilitate (we dare not say 'enforce') in order to be termed Cooperative Learning.

Catch1Partner

Catch1Partner is a seven-step CLIP. The teacher issues materials, sets a task and all the learners execute the following action steps:

1. Learners mingle quietly, holding up materials until they find a partner.

2. Partner A poses his/her question.

3. Partner B answers.

4. Partner A praises, thanks or helps.

5. Partners switch roles.

6. Partners swap materials.*

7. Partners bid farewell and proceed from step 1.

* Step 6 is left out in activities where materials are personalised. We saw this in Activity 4 (see page 61), where each learner is hunting for answers to their list of questions, and the initial stages of the German MFL lessons described in Activity 5 (see page 69), where individual students were made responsible for transmitting the pronunciation of their verbs.

The four basic rules of staging an activity

These four basic rules detail the direct instruction required for learners to successfully execute a CLIP:

1. Scaffold the subject task.
2. Be specific about what you want them to do.
3. Show, don't tell.
4. Ask instruction-checking questions.

Note that the more consistently you use a CLIP, the shorter the staging process. For the simple revision of familiar materials, setting a class off should take no more than a few seconds, excluding the time to distribute materials. However, when you make changes to materials and/or substantially alter the tasks that partners are going to perform, these rules apply. It is the teacher's responsibility to set the learners up to succeed, and you know best how much support is needed in each situation.

The silence signal

We have identified the silence signal as good practice when switching between peer and teacher engagement, but use whatever system works for you.

The instructions to your learners are as follows:

When teacher lifts his hand:

1. Lift yours.
2. Be quiet.
3. Where relevant, put down any pens.
4. Look at the teacher and listen (and maybe gently help an inattentive friend to do the same).

Appendix F
Word-Round Transcript from a Key Stage 2 Maths Lesson

This transcript is from a Word-Round in a Year 5 maths lesson where the lesson objective was to use multiplication and division to answer word problems. For Word-Round, learners are ideally seated in teams of four. We have included the teacher's modelling so you can see how the link between the modelling and the Cooperative Learning Interaction Pattern was attained, as well as the importance of direct instruction.

Teacher [*reading the question from the board and modelling*]: Forty-five pizzas are cut into 8 slices each. They are shared between 60 people. How many slices does each person get?

So, I have read the question and now I need to think about what I have to do. I'm going to have to divide something as it says 'share'. Turn to the person next to you and say: 'Share means divide.'

[*The children do this and the teacher resumes, drawing and writing on the board as he speaks*] Teacher: If I am going to share 'something' by 60, I will need to find what I am sharing 60 by.

First, I know there are 45 whole pizzas and each of these is split into 8 equal slices, so one pizza will have 8 slices or one lot of 8.

I know that this is multiplication. Two whole pizzas will have 16 because I know that 2 lots of 8, or 2 x 8, is equal to 16.

I need to do 45 x 8. I know that 5 lots of 8 are 40 [*quickly rote counts in 8s five times*]. I also know that 40 lots of 8 are 320; I know this because 4 x 8 = 32. I then add 40 and 320 together, which is 360 because 32 + 4 = 36. [*Notes are made on the board clearly in front of all*]

In a Word-Round, explain how I have arrived at 360 – you have 25 seconds each. Start with person 2.[1] One, two, three, go! *[The teacher launches loop timer and walks around the class listening]*

[Recorded dialogue (four mixed-ability children)]

Person 1:   *[Prompts]* *[Name]*, you're person 2! Miss said your corner starts!

Person 2:   Err, Miss said … was that you look at the question … and we know that there's like 45 pizzas, and that made me hungry, and that it had be cut into, like 8, and that all the pizzas had to be shared between people and that she didn't know how to share it with everyone. So she did 45 x 8 and got 360 because five 8s are 40 and 40 eights are 320, so she added those together.

Person 3:   I agree … We needed to find the number so we could divide it by 60 and that five 8s are 40 and that because four 8s are 32 we multiplied that by 10 so it's 32 x 10 which is 320. And then we added the 40, which is 5 lots, and that gave us 360, so we will have to divide that by 60 …

Person 4:   That's how she got 360 *[starts drawing in the air]* … I'd have like used a column method and put the 8 under the 5 and done eight 5s are 40 and written down a 0, then carried the 4 then done four 8s and added … 4 so … 36 and it gives 360.

Person 1:   Yeah … I'd have did all that … so it's look at the numbers you need to multiply, so it's 45 and 8 and it's 360 and … 40 x 8 is 320 because it's 4 x 8 add a 0, and like 5 and 8 is 40 *[holds up fingers and quickly counts 5, 10, 15, 20, 25, 30, 35, 40]* … and then we've got to divide it by 60 …

Teacher *[addressing whole class]*: Some clear use of language and a range of methods heard as I was walking around. Now, I have 360 which I have to divide by 60 as 360 was the product of 45 and 8. Remember: *product* is the answer of a multiplication sum; turn to the person next to you and say: 'The product is the answer of a multiplication sum.'

[The children do this and the teacher resumes] Teacher: I now need to divide by 60 as 360. There are many ways of doing this, but I know that 36 is equal to 6 multiplied by 6. Therefore, I know that if I make 6 ten times bigger it will

---

1   Pupils are seated in teams of four and each of the four team members have a designator (e.g. 1s, 2s, 3s, 4s; Giraffes, Lions, Elephants, Zebras; Reds, Greens, Blues, Yellows) which allows the teacher to micromanage all the teams simultaneously across the class. The command: 'Reds, pick up the materials from my desk!' sees all the Reds, one from each team, stand up, get the materials and return to their teams to distribute. In a Cooperative Learning classroom we do things for our team because the teacher has better things to do than run around with handouts.

be 60 x 6 which is 360. If I use the inverse, 360 divided by 60 is 6. So I've used two steps to solve this [returns to the question]: 45 pizzas are sliced into 8 slices each – that was 360. They (the 360) are shared between 60 people. How many slices does each person get? They get 6 slices.

Each team is now issued with a similar word problem. For this group the question was: 'I have 84 marbles. I keep 19 for myself and share the rest between five friends. How many marbles do they each get?' Following three minutes of individual work on the question, a new Word-Round was launched with each member speaking for 25 seconds, this time starting with Person 1:

Person 1:   So we have to find out how many marbles the friends get – I got 16 [disagreement hand signal used by three on the table] coz, no [laughs] … when I did 5s into 84 I got 16 when I counted on my fingers … and there's sixteen 5s in 84 and there's some marbles left …

Person 2:   I don't think that that's like right ['agree' hand signals from persons 3 and 4] because … you need to take 19 away from 84 first – that's … err 65! Coz I did a column method … Then you do 6s … no, 5s into 65 which is 13.

Person 3:   I took away 19 from 84, which is take away 20 and add 1 … [looking at person 2's notes]. Errr … I did a bus stop for that bit [points at $65 \div 5 = 13$] … then … did 5 into 1 goes 1 remainder 1 … then did 5 into 15 that's 3, so its 13 [agreement hand signals]. Coz it is …

Person 4:   I agree that it's 13, not like 16. But I did that 10 lots of 5 is 50 and then 3 lots of 5 is 15 and so together I got 13, but I had to start with 84 and take away 19 … I did column for that bit [points at paper].

Interestingly, person 4 rejects some the statements by persons 1 and 2, not for the accuracy of their answers but for the method at which they had been arrived. The children did not wish to use a prescribed method – that is, the one modelled by the teacher – but instead chose their own path.

In general, there are two interesting things to note: one was that the teacher did not ask the whole class questions during their modelling, and the second concerns the dialogue in which the children were involved. All of them were engaged in the CLIP and adapted their explanations to fit the timescales the teacher had set out.

Bibliography

Adams, D. (1995 [1980]) *The Restaurant at the End of the Universe* (The Hitchhiker's Guide to the Galaxy series, vol. 2). New York: Del Rey.

Allison, S. and Tharby, A. (2015) *Making Every Lesson Count: Six Principles to Support Great Teaching and Learning*. Carmarthen: Crown House Publishing.

Barber, S. J., Rajaram, S. and Fox, E. B. (2012) Learning and Remembering with Others: The Key Role of Retrieval in Shaping Group Recall and Collective Memory. *Social Cognition*, 30(1): 121–132. DOI:10.1521/soco.2012.30.1.121

Caper, G. and Tarim, K. (2015) Efficacy of the Cooperative Learning Method on Mathematics Achievement and Attitude: A Meta-Analysis Research. *Educational Sciences: Theory & Practice*, 15(2): 553–559. DOI:10.12738/estp.2015.2.2098

Carpenter, S. K. and Agarwal, P. K. (2020) *How to Use Spaced Retrieval Practice to Boost Learning*. Ames, IA: Iowa State University. Available at: http://pdf.retrievalpractice.org/SpacingGuide.pdf.

Cohen, E. and Lotan, R. (2014) *Designing Group Work: Strategies for Heterogeneous Classrooms*. New York: Teachers College Press.

Corbett, P. and Strong, J. (n.d.) The Talk for Writing Process. Available at: http://www.talk4writing.co.uk/wp-content/uploads/2015/04/T4W-overview-expanded.pdf.

Cranney, J., Ahn, M., McKinnon, R., Morris, S. and Watts, K. (2009) The Testing Effect, Collaborative Learning, and Retrieval-Induced Facilitation in a Classroom Setting. *European Journal of Cognitive Psychology*, 21(6): 919–940.

Creemers, B. P. M. and Kyriakides, L. (2008) *The Dynamics of Educational Effectiveness: A Contribution to Policy, Practice and Theory in Contemporary Schools*. Abingdon: Routledge.

Department for Children, Schools and Families (2008) *Personalised Learning: A Practical Guide*. Nottingham: DCSF. Available at: https://dera.ioe.ac.uk/8447/7/00844-2008DOM-EN_Redacted.pdf.

Di Pietro, G., Biagi, F., Costa, P., Karpiński, Z. and Mazza, J. (2020) *The Likely Impact of COVID-19 on Education: Reflections Based on the Existing Literature and Recent International Datasets*. Luxembourg: Publications Office of the European Union. Available at: https://publications.jrc.ec.europa.eu/repository/bitstream/JRC121071/jrc121071.pdf.

Dicken, J. (2020) The Cost of Lockdown: Attainment Gap Widens By Up to 52% for Primary Pupils. *Schools Week* (24 July). Available at: https://schoolsweek.co.uk/the-cost-of-lockdown-attainment-gap-widens-by-up-to-52-for-primary-pupils.

Dufrene, B., Lestremau, L. and Zoder-Martell, K. (2014) Direct Behavioral Consultation: Effects on Teachers' Praise and Student Disruptive Behavior. *Psychology in the Schools*, 51(6): 567–580.

Education Endowment Foundation (2018a) Collaborative Learning (13 November). Available at: https://educationendowmentfoundation.org.uk/evidence-summaries/teaching-learning-toolkit/collaborative-learning.

Education Endowment Foundation (2018b) Feedback (28 September). Available at: https://educationendowmentfoundation.org.uk/evidence-summaries/teaching-learning-toolkit/feedback.

Education Endowment Foundation (2018c) Metacognition and Self-Regulated Learning (30 August). Available at: https://educationendowmentfoundation.org.uk/evidence-summaries/teaching-learning-toolkit/meta-cognition-and-self-regulation.

Education Endowment Foundation (2019) Oral Language Interventions (20 September). Available at: https://educationendowmentfoundation.org.uk/evidence-summaries/teaching-learning-toolkit/oral-language-interventions.

Fadel, C. (2008) *21st Century Skills: How Can You Prepare Students for the New Global Economy?* Paris: Organisation for Economic Co-operation and Development/Centre for Educational Research and Innovation. Available at: https://www.oecd.org/site/educeri21st/40756908.pdf.

Fernyhough, C. (2016) *The Voices Within: The History and Science of How We Talk to Ourselves*. New York: Basic Books.

Gibbons, P. (2002) *Scaffolding Language, Scaffolding Learning: Teaching Second Language Learners in the Mainstream Classroom*. Portsmouth, NH: Heinemann Educational Books.

Glossary of Education Reform (2016) 21st Century Skills (25 August). Available at: https://www.edglossary.org/21st-century-skills.

Halliday, M. (1993) Towards a Language-Based Theory of Learning. *Linguistics and Education*, 5(2): 93–116.

Hattie, J. (2009) *Visible Learning: A Synthesis of Meta-Analysis Relating to Achievement*. Abingdon and New York: Routledge.

Hook, P. (2016) *First Steps with SOLO Taxonomy: Applying the Model in Your Classroom*. Invercargill: Essential Resources Educational Publishers.

Howard-Jones, P., Varma, S., Ansari, D. and Butterworth, B. (2016) The Principles and Practices of Educational Neuroscience: Commentary on Bowers. *Psychological Review*, 123(5): 620–627.

Izumo, K., Saito, D. and Sadato, N. (2008) Processing of Social and Monetary Rewards in the Human Striatum. *Neuron*, 58(2): 284–294.

Johnson, R. T. and Johnson, D. W. (1994) An Overview of Cooperative Learning. In J. Thousand, A. Villa and A. Nevin (eds), *Creativity and Collaborative Learning*. Baltimore, MD: Brookes Press, pp. 1–21.

Johnson, R. T. and Johnson, D. W. (1999) *Joining Together: Group Theory and Group Skills*. Englewood Cliffs, NJ: Prentice Hall.

Johnson, R. T., Johnson, D. W. and Holubec, E. (1991) *Cooperation in the Classroom*, rev. edn. Edina, MN: Interaction Book Co.

Jolliffe, W. (2005) The Implementation of Cooperative Learning in the Classroom. Paper presented at the British Educational Research Association Annual Conference, University of Glamorgan, 14–17 September.

Kagan, S. (1998) Staff Development and the Structural Approach to Cooperative Learning. In C. M. Brody, N. Davidson and C. Cooper, *Professional Development for Cooperative Learning: Issues and Approaches*. New York: Teachers College Press, pp. 103–123.

Kirschner, F., Paas, F. and Kirschner, P. A. (2011) Task Complexity as a Driver for Collaborative Learning Efficiency: The Collective Working-Memory Effect. *Applied Cognitive Psychology*, 25(4): 615–624.

Kirschner, A., Sweller, J. and Clark, R. E. (2006) Why Minimal Guidance During Instruction Does Not Work: An Analysis of the Failure of Constructivist, Discovery, Problem-Based, Experiential, and Inquiry-Based Teaching. *Educational Psychologist*, 41(2): 75–86. DOI:10.1207/s15326985ep4102_1

Kirschner, P. A., Sweller, J., Kirschner, F. and Zambrano, J. (2018) From Cognitive Load Theory to Collaborative Cognitive Load Theory. *International Journal of Computer-Supported Collaborative Learning*, 13(2): 213–233.

Kutnick, P. and Blatchford, P. (2014) *Effective Group Work in Primary School Classrooms*. New York: Springer-Verlag.

Laal, M. and Ghodsi, S. M. (2011) Benefits of Collaborative Learning. *Procedia – Social and Behavioral Sciences*, 31: 486-490. DOI:10.1016/j.sbspro.2011.12.091

Lane, S. (2016) Promoting Collaborative Learning Among Students. *American Journal of Educational Research*, 4(8): 602–607. DOI: 10.12691/education-4-8-4

Lough, C. (2020) Wide Variation in School Teaching Assistant Spend. *TES* (27 February). Available at: https://www.tes.com/news/wide-variation-school-teaching-assistant-spend.

Lyman, F. (1981) The Responsive Classroom Discussion. In A. S. Anderson (ed.), *Mainstreaming Digest*. College Park, MD: University of Maryland College of Education, pp. 109–113.

McAlister, C. (2010) Cooperative Learning in Scotland: Perspectives on the Role of Cooperative Learning in Supporting Curricular Policy and Innovation. Paper presented at the European Conference on Educational Research, Helsinki, Finland, 23–27 August.

Maxwell, B., Burnett, C., Reidy, J., Willis, B. and Demack, S. (2015) *Oracy Curriculum, Culture and Assessment Toolkit: Evaluation Report and Executive Summary*. London: Education Endowment Foundation. Available at: http://shura.shu.ac.uk/10828/1/EEF%20Oracy%20School_21.pdf.

Mello, R. R. (2012) From Constructivism to Dialogism in the Classroom: Theory and Learning Environments. *International Journal of Education Psychology*, 1(2): 127–152.

Mercer, N. (1995) *The Guided Construction of Knowledge: Talk Amongst Teachers and Learners*. Clevedon: Multilingual Matters.

Mevarech, Z. (1985) The Effects of Cooperative Mastery Learning Strategies on Mathematics Achievement. *Journal of Educational Research*, 78(6): 372–377.

Millis, B. (2008) Enhancing Learning – and More! – Through Cooperative Learning. Idea Paper #38. Available at: https://www.ideaedu.org/Portals/0/Uploads/Documents/IDEA%20Papers/IDEA%20Papers/IDEA_Paper_38.pdf.

Millis, B. (2012) *Cooperative Learning in Higher Education: Across the Disciplines, Across the Academy*. Sterling, VA: Stylus Publishing.

Mineo, L. (2017) Good Genes Are Nice, But Joy Is Better. *Harvard Gazette* (11 April). Available at: https://news.harvard.edu/gazette/story/2017/04/over-nearly-80-years-harvard-study-has-been-showing-how-to-live-a-healthy-and-happy-life.

Muijs, D. and Reynolds, D. (2017) *Effective Teaching, Evidence and Practice*, 4th edn. Thousand Oaks, CA: SAGE.

National Literacy Trust (2019) *Language Unlocks Reading: Supporting Early Language and Reading for Every Child*. Available at: https://cdn.literacytrust.org.uk/media/documents/Language_unlocks_reading.pdf.

Newman, F. M. and Thompson, J. (1987) *Effects of Cooperative Learning on Achievement in Secondary Schools: A Summary of Research*. Madison, WI: University of Wisconsin/National Center on Effective Secondary Schools.

Ofsted (2016a) School Report: Henderson Green Primary Academy (20–21 November). Available at: https://files.ofsted.gov.uk/v1/file/50049537.

Ofsted (2016b) School Report: Stalham Academy (24–25 November). Available at: https://files.ofsted.gov.uk/v1/file/2634323.

Ofsted (2019a) *Education Inspection Framework: Overview of Research* (January). Ref: 180045. Available at: https://assets.publishing.service.gov.uk/government/uploads/system/uploads/attachment_data/file/926364/Research_for_EIF_framework_100619__16_.pdf.

Ofsted (2019b) *School Inspection Handbook* [draft] (January). Ref: 180041. Available at: https://assets.publishing.service.gov.uk/government/uploads/system/uploads/attachment_data/file/801615/Schools_draft_handbook_180119_archived.pdf.

Ofsted (2019c) *School Inspection Update: January 2019, Special Edition*. Available at: https://assets.publishing.service.gov.uk/government/uploads/system/uploads/attachment_data/file/772056/School_inspection_update_-_January_2019_Special_Edition_180119.pdf.

Ofsted (2020) Children Hardest Hit By COVID-19 Pandemic Are Regressing in Basic Skills and Learning (10 November) [press release]. Available at: https://www.gov.uk/government/news/ofsted-children-hardest-hit-by-covid-19-pandemic-are-regressing-in-basic-skills-and-learning.

Oracy All-Party Parliamentary Group (2020) *Speak for Change: Initial Findings and Recommendations from the Oracy All-Party Parliamentary Group Inquiry* (December). Available at: https://d5119182-bdac-43d5-be55-e817e7736e5b.filesusr.com/ugd/2c80ff_33e3208ce4dd4764b154682488c53ef7.pdf.

Pisapia, J. and Westfall, A. (1994) Developing Resilient Schools and Resilient Students. Research Brief #19. Richmond, VA: Metropolitan Educational Research Consortium.

Poortvliet, M. V., Clarke, A. and Gross, J. (2019) *Improving Social and Emotional Learning in Primary Schools: Guidance Report.* London: Education Endowment Foundation and Early Intervention Foundation. Available at: https://educationendowmentfoundation.org.uk/public/files/Publications/SEL/EEF_Social_and_Emotional_Learning.pdf.

Quigley, A., Muijs, D. and Stringer, E. (2018) *Metacognition and Self-Regulated Learning: Guidance Report.* London: Education Endowment Foundation. Available at: https://educationendowmentfoundation.org.uk/public/files/Publications/Metacognition/EEF_Metacognition_and_self-regulated_learning.pdf.

Raffaele, L. M. and Knoff, H. M. (1999) Improving Home–School Collaboration with Disadvantaged Families: Organisational Principles, Perspectives, and Approaches. *School Psychology Review*, 28(3): 448–466.

Rethink (2019) Largest Survey of Its Kind Reveals Extent of University Students' Struggles with Thoughts of Self-Harm, Loneliness and Anxiety (5 March). Available at: https://www.rethink.org/news-and-stories/news/2019/mar/largest-survey-of-its-kind-reveals-extent-of-university-students-struggles-with-thoughts-of-self-harm-loneliness-and-anxiety.

Rogers, B. (2018) *The Big Ideas in Physics and How to Teach Them: Teaching Physics 11–18.* Abingdon and New York: Routledge.

Rosenshine, B. (2012) Principles of Instruction: Research-Based Strategies That All Teachers Should Know. *American Educator* (spring): 12–19, 39. Available at: https://www.aft.org/sites/default/files/periodicals/Rosenshine.pdf.

Sharples, J., Webster, R. and Blatchford, P. (2015) *Making Best Use of Teaching Assistants: Guidance Report.* London: Education Endowment Foundation. Available at: https://educationendowmentfoundation.org.uk/public/files/Publications/Teaching_Assistants/TA_Guidance_Report_MakingBestUseOfTeachingAssistants-Printable.pdf.

Sherrington, T. (2019) *Rosenshine's Principles in Action.* Woodbridge: John Catt Educational.

Soderstrom, N. C. and Bjork, R. A. (2015) Learning Versus Performance: An Integrative Review. *Perspectives on Psychological Science*, 10(2): 176–199.

Sutherland, K., Wehby, J. and Copeland, S. (2000) Effect of Varying Rates of Behavior-Specific Praise on the On-Task Behavior of Students with EBD. *Journal of Emotional and Behavioral Disorders*, 8(1): 2–8.

Sweller, J., Ayres, P. and Kalyuga, S. (2011) *Cognitive Load Theory.* New York: Springer.

van Leeuwen, A. and Janssen, J. (2019) Learning in Primary and Secondary Education. *Educational Research Review*, 27: 71–89.

van Ryzin, M. J., and Roseth, C. J. (2018) Cooperative Learning in Middle School: A Means to Improve Peer Relations and Reduce Victimization, Bullying, and Related Outcomes. *Journal of Educational Psychology*, 110(8): 1192–1201. DOI:10.1037/edu0000265

Vygotsky, L. (1978) *Mind in Society: The Development of Higher Psychological Processes.* Cambridge, MA: Harvard University Press.

Werdelin, J. (n.d.) 'Mum Wasn't Good at Maths Either, Love …' Girls, Maths & Cooperative Learning in the Norfolk SSIF Bid. *cooperativelearning.works.* Available at: https://cooperativelearning.works/mum-wasnt-good-at-maths-either-love-girls-maths-cooperative-learning-in-the-norfolk-ssif-bid.

Werdelin, J. (2014a) Better (Talk4)Writing Through Cooperative Learning. *cooperativelearning.works* (26 April). Available at: https://cooperativelearning.works/2016/04/26/better-talk4writing-through-cooperative-learning/#more-4086.

Werdelin, J. (2014b) Deconstructing the Progressive–Traditional Dichotomy; A Note to Mr Peal. *cooperativelearning.works* (26 December). Available at: https://cooperativelearning.works/2014/12/26/deconstructing-the-progressive-traditional-dichotomy-a-note-to-mr-peal.

Werdelin, J. (2015a) Inside Out? Collaborating Introverts. *cooperativelearning.works* (5 October). Available at: https://cooperativelearning.works/2015/10/05/inside-out-collaborating-introverts.

Werdelin, J. (2015b) Tertiary in the 21st Century: A Cooperative Learning Toolkit [video interview with Professor Lee Marsden]. Available at: https://videos.werdelin.co.uk/#collection/13.

Werdelin, J. (2017a) Cooperative Learning; Closed Questions, Closed Achievement Gaps. *cooperativelearning.works* (26 May). Available at: https://cooperativelearning.works/2017/05/26/cooperative-learning-closed-questions-closed-achievement-gaps.

Werdelin, J. (2017b) Making Best Use of … Leadership; Coaching & Cooperative Learning. *cooperativelearning.works* (20 September). Available at: https://cooperativelearning.works/2017/09/20/making-best-use-of-leadership-coaching-cooperative-learning.

Werdelin, J. (2018a) A Piece of Cake: Stuart Kime on Baking Your Own Research Network. *cooperativelearning.works* (19 September). Available at: https://cooperativelearning.works/2018/09/19/a-piece-of-cake-stuart-kime-on-baking-your-own-research-network.

Werdelin, J. (2018b) So Far, So Good. *cooperativelearning.works* (8 March). Available at: https://cooperativelearning.works/2018/03/08/so-far-so-good.

Werdelin, J. (2019a) 'Don't Worry, Dad … Now I Can Teach You Maths!' – the Success of the Gender Gap SSIF. *cooperativelearning.works* (11 June). Available at: https://cooperativelearning.works/2019/06/11/dont-worry-dad-now-i-can-teach-you-maths-the-success-of-the-gender-gap-ssif.

Werdelin, J. (2019b) In a Word: Co-Creative Conversation Explained. *cooperativelearning.works* (29 April). Available at: https://cooperativelearning.works/2019/04/29/in-a-word-co-creative-conversation-explained.

Werdelin, J. (2019c) Participatory Budgeting in Schools? #1; The Stakes and the Stakeholders. *cooperativelearning.works* (20 February). Available at: https://cooperativelearning.works/2019/02/20/participatory-budgeting-in-schools-1-the-stakes-and-the-stakeholders.

Werdelin, J. (2019d) Participatory Budgeting in Schools #10: Q&A with Sean Harford Pt. 1. *cooperativelearning.works* (29 June). Available at: https://cooperativelearning.works/2019/06/29/participatory-budgeting-in-schools-10-qa-with-sean-harford.

Werdelin, J. (2019e) Widening Participation; How Cooperative Learning Can Put Possible Selves into Practice. *cooperativelearning.works* (27 October). Available at: https://cooperativelearning.works/2019/10/27/widening-participation-how-cooperative-learning-can-put-possible-selves-into-practice.

Wolfe, S. and Alexander, R. J. (2008) *Argumentation and Dialogic Teaching: Alternative Pedagogies for a Changing World*. London: Futurelab. Available at: http://robinalexander.org.uk/wp-content/uploads/2019/12/wolfealexander.pdf.

Yamarik, S. (2010) Does Cooperative Learning Improve Student Learning Outcomes? *Journal of Economic Education*, 38(3): 259–277.

Zakaria, E., Solfitri, T., Daud, Y. and Abidin, Z. Z. (2013) Effect of Cooperative Learning on Secondary School Students' Mathematics Achievement. *Creative Education*, 4(2): 98–100.

Index